HELPING MOTHERS BE CLOSER TO THEIR SONS

Understanding the unique world of boys

HELPING MOTHERS BE CLOSER TO THEIR SONS

Understanding the unique world of boys

Tom Golden, LCSW

G.H. Publishing, LLC PO Box 83658 Gaithersburg, Maryland 20878   Copyright 2016, G.H. Publishing, L.L.C.   All rights reserved. No part of this book may be reproduced or transmitted in any form or by any means, electronic or mechanical, including photocopying, recording, or by any information storage and retrieval system, without permission in writing from the author.

TABLE OF CONTENTS

Preface	**vii**
Introduction	**1**
IT STARTS EARLY	**3**
The Testosterone Flood	3
Systemizing	7
What we talk about	7
A Thousand Shades of Grey	9
Male-Male Competition	12
Daily Competing	19
Differences in Ways of Getting What You Want	22
Play	24
Precarious Manhood	27
Getting Close to Boys - Where are His Feelings?	**33**
Male Pain is Ignored	35
Socialization	37
Biology and Emotions	39
Transmen	41
Getting Close to Boys - How Does He Heal?	**45**
Telling the Story	48
Michael Jordan and Practical Action	56
Applying this to your son	60
Getting Close to Boys	**65**
Storytelling	70
Telling stories where you make them a part	72
Telling stories as a group	73
Stories for Older Adolescents	73

Learn from him about his sport	*74*
Compete with him	*74*
Going to bed	*75*
Coming Home From School	*75*

BOYS AND DISCIPLINE — 79
Know what the rules are — *80*
Go with positive reinforcement when you can — *82*
Challenge him — *83*
Give him as much responsibility as you can — *83*
Use his interest in competition — *84*

ADOLESCENCE — 87

BOYS AND EMOTIONS — Some tips — 89

Summary and Resources — 93

References — 97

About the Author — 103

Preface

This book is not meant to be a hard and fast handbook of boys. When you read these pages you will likely see that some of the ideas will fit your son and some will not. That is the beauty of human beings. We are remarkably diverse and there is no right or wrong way and not even a strict "boys way" or "girls way." It's much more complicated with many shades of grey. The hope is that you will use this book to see your son's uniqueness. Knowing his distinctive qualities will be a big help in getting close. Your job is to see how your son is different and love him for it.

Boys and girls experiences are often very different. The first section of this book will describe a number of these differences, the main three being the testosterone flood in utero, male to male competition, and precarious manhood. Each of these has a profound impact on your son and probably not on your daughters. Each of these are relatively unknown. The second section will explain how boys react to these three factors. This section starts by discussing the how and why of boys' <u>invisible emotions</u> and follows with a discussion of the many ways that boys and men do heal. Again, their ways to heal are often invisible to the untrained eye, which leaves us at risk of unnecessary judgments. Imagine that your way to heal was not seen or acknowledged. It would likely leave you feeling distant and misunderstood, right? Closeness would be unlikely. By knowing boys' ways of healing, you will be able to understand them and sometimes join them in their healing. We all know that healing moments are one factor that builds closeness. When you are able to see the cloaking and the alternative healing paths you are in a much better position to be understanding and gain emotional closeness. Women often feel relieved when they can make sense of the ways boys and men process emotions. We will then spend some time looking at other ways to feel close with your son based on these differences, examine some ideas about discipline and offer tips about teaching him about emotions.

Let's get started.

Introduction

This is a book for women who love their sons and want to increase their emotional closeness with them. You might wonder why there is a need for such a book. The answer is that there is a great deal of information about boys and men that simply never hits the media or even our educational system. This leaves us not knowing important information about our boys. This book will give you a good start in understanding how your boys are unique. It will also give you resources for further study in case you would like to learn more about these issues.

Women are very aware of what it was like growing up in a female body. They know about what their experience was like being a girl and the obvious and the subtle things that girls do. They have a good idea of what might motivate them, drive them nuts, what they might dream of, how they relate, how they fight and much, much more. But women, understandably, don't know these things about their sons.

This book is designed to help you get a sense of the range of experiences of being male and especially the experiences of being a young boy. When we have clues about our sons' unique experiences we are in a better position to know how to motivate them, to know what they want and how they want it, to speak their language, to know what is underneath some of their

Helping Mothers Be Closer to Their Sons

decisions that might seem bizarre, and of course, to be close to them. By knowing their nature we are in a better position to connect.

In my work as a therapist I have repeatedly seen mothers who love their sons but take approaches that work very well with their daughters but not so well with their sons. This tends to create more distance rather than closeness and leaves moms frustrated. The moms want the best for their sons but not knowing his nature leaves them at a disadvantage and probably frustrated. The hope is that this book will help you avoid that sort of frustration by having a greater awareness of your son's nature whether it is the way he heals, the way he emotes or even his response to being disciplined. This book will help you along that path.

As a mom you know better than anyone about your son's uniqueness. I hope you can let this book open you to some research driven ideas that may bring that understanding up a notch and facilitate an even deeper closeness.

IT STARTS EARLY

The differences between boys and girls start very early. In fact they start the first day of life. Research has shown that infant boys are more likely to attend to an object or a mobile while infant girls are more likely to attend to a human face.[1] But why this difference so shortly after birth? With no socialization to influence boys or girls at day one how is it that there might be differences? This is where we need to back up about 6 or 7 months.

The Testosterone Flood

At approximately eight weeks in utero most boys receive what is called a testosterone flood. This sudden increase in testosterone has multiple consequences. One consequence is that these raised levels of testosterone change the brain of the baby. The default brain is the female brain or what researcher Simon Baron-Cohen calls the "relational" or "empathic" brain.[2] This relational brain is built to focus more on empathy, nurturing and relationships. Without the testosterone flood we would all have this relational brain, but with the flood, the brain starts to develop into what researchers call the male brain or what Baron-Cohen calls the "systemizing brain." This male brain has a different set of strengths. It prefers to focus on systems: what makes them tick, what removing one

Helping Mothers Be Closer to Their Sons

piece might do to the whole, what a simple change in one part might do to another, the joy of building it piece by piece or taking it apart. Think Legos. Can you remember little boys spending hours upon hours with Legos? I bet you can. I would also bet that you might remember a similarly aged little girl that loved Legos in about the same way. And here is where things get interesting. It turns out that an estimated 17% of females also get an increase in testosterone in utero and develop what researchers call male brains.[3] The girls who get this testosterone tend to be much less interested in traditionally feminine sorts of things, they would rather play rough and climb trees and spend hours with Legos. They tend to feel more happy being with the boys and they will often reject ostensibly female things. What we know now is that these young ladies are unique as girls at least in part because they got this extra testosterone and it is this pre-natal testosterone that is playing a part. I'm sure you have known some of these girls before; we call them "Tom Boys."

It's important to note that an estimated 17% of boys do not get this testosterone flood and therefore have a more "female" brain. These are the boys that are easier for moms to understand. They are more like mom and their way of being in the world is more like mom is used to. If you have a son like this (and if you have a "female brain") you may be close due to your similarity. This is the young man that makes you wonder why your other sons can't be like that.

Researchers have been able to identify those boys and girls who experienced this extra testosterone and they have studied these boy's and girl's behaviors and personalities as they have gotten older. What they have found is that those with greater

It Starts Early

testosterone levels in utero are more likely to want to play with "boy" toys like trucks and things that move. They are more likely to be more active, aggressive and competitive, less interested in traditionally feminine things and less interested in infants and nurturing behaviors.[4,5] Those with lower levels of testosterone are more likely to have more interest in dolls and playing house, to be more interested in nurturing and in sharing secrets and personal data, and to prefer to play with a single friend or two rather than with a larger group. Of course parents have been seeing these differences for a long time but likely assumed these differences were based solely on socialization, not on biology. Now we know differently. There are many factors that impact our differences.

A good deal of research is being done on the testosterone flood and how it influences children. As of 2015, scientists are confident about four connected differences from this flood. These are the boy-typical play behaviors, the increased chance of aggressive behavior, influence on the core sexual identity and an impact on sexual orientation.[6] There are other differences that are being studied but the strength of connection has yet to be proven for these.

What does this tell us? It suggests that your son, if he had the testosterone flood, will probably like to play in a way that most boys like to play, he may be interested in masculine play and be turned off by feminine activity. He will likely be attracted to females when he matures and he may be aggressive at times.

Our personalities are impacted by our biology even before we are born. This goes against common knowledge that our socialization is the only determinant to our ways of being. This is false. Our prenatal testosterone is just one biological factor and it impacts us in a profound manner. This testosterone flood has what biologists call "organizational" qualities. That is, the testosterone organizes the brain in certain patterns, literally changing the brain's structure.[7] These patterns make up what is being called the male brain. In addition to testosterone's organizational qualities it also sensitizes receptor cells in the brain to be more reactive so that later in life the bodies of the boys and girls who received this flood will be more reactive to testosterone. This is called testosterone priming. Lastly, testosterone has what scientists call activational qualities. These are more transient and non-permanent effects on an already developed nervous system. This is what most of us think of when we think of hormones and the way they work. We get a squirt of this or that hormone and our bodies react accordingly.

Prenatal testosterone is not the only time when there is a surge in testosterone within boys' bodies. A second surge of testosterone happens shortly after baby boys are born. Some scientists are calling this the "Mini Puberty."[8] This surge lasts between the first to third month of life (and sometimes longer) and is being studied now to get a sense of what impact it might have on these young boys. This surge is considerably easier to study since direct measurements of the testosterone can be made on a regular basis and do not depend on the blood levels of the pregnant mother or the testosterone levels in the amniotic fluid.

And, of course, there is the flood of testosterone that we are all familiar with, when boys reach puberty and once again

It Starts Early

their bodies are flooded with testosterone, about ten to twenty times the levels of testosterone that their sisters experience.

SYSTEMIZING

Let's take just a minute to examine what is meant by the systemizing brain that seems to result from the testosterone flood. This systemizing brain prefers to focus on systems. But when we say systems, what do we mean? These systems might be about anything with an input and an output. An example might be a machine like a car. It has numerous driver "inputs" like steering, braking, and accelerating. Change one of the inputs and the system changes. Learning how these inputs change the outputs is learning the system. A mainframe computer would be a more complex example. Or take a simpler example like Legos, there are a multitude of ways to attach the pieces, different colors, and different shapes. Learning the system is learning how to manipulate the inputs to get the output you might want. Another system might be swinging a baseball bat. The swing itself is a system. Learning the different parts of the swing, learning how to adjust that swing, and various different 'inputs" the ball player could use to get the desired outputs is a system. Systems can even be as simple as a phonebook where names and numbers are connected or as complex as a philosophy. Our worlds are filled with systems.

WHAT WE TALK ABOUT

An easy way to get a sense of this difference in the systemizing brain and the empathic brain is to think for a moment about the

Helping Mothers Be Closer to Their Sons

topics of conversations of your sons and of your daughters. What sorts of things do your sons like to talk about? I would bet that they talk about systems or competing, and sometimes both. Talking about video games is talking about systems: input and output and which inputs bring success. Boys can talk about video games for hours. What was done, what worked, what didn't, and all the gory details of the experience. (Of course they would prefer to play them and not talk.) I am willing to bet you have heard these conversations before. Discussing sports is another system: who is winning, what Team A needs to do to be more competitive against Team B, and on and on. The other piece is that in both these topics there is a likelihood that the discussion centered around competition. Who is first? Second? Last? Who is a level up and who is five levels behind? And this of course is a part of the system.

Now contrast this with the typical discussion you might hear with girls. Sure the girls might talk about sports or video games but it seems more likely they will talk about relationships. Who is their best friend, what are they doing together? Who will or won't play with whom? Disclosing this or that personal data. Hearing about others' relationships. This is what you are more likely to hear from your girls. Some girls, however, will love to talk about sports and some boys will be more interested in relationships. What we are talking about is not a predictor of behavior but is a way of observing it. You can't say, "Because he is a boy, he will do this or that." But you can simply observe how your child may or may not fit in with the differences we are describing and build a deeper understanding of their uniqueness. Once we observe we can see how this plays out in the lives of our children.

It Starts Early

A THOUSAND SHADES OF GREY

These differences are not black and white. As we have noted, it is simply untrue to claim that all boys will be one way and all girls another. It is much more complicated and subtle than that. These differences are usually in degrees. Think about this, boys are taller than girls. That statement is similar to the ones we are making about male and female brains above but let's look closely at it. The truth is that most boys are taller than most girls. You will have a few girls who are taller than most boys and some boys who are shorter than most girls, but the majority of the boys are *usually* taller than the majority of girls. You can look at a chart to see how this works.

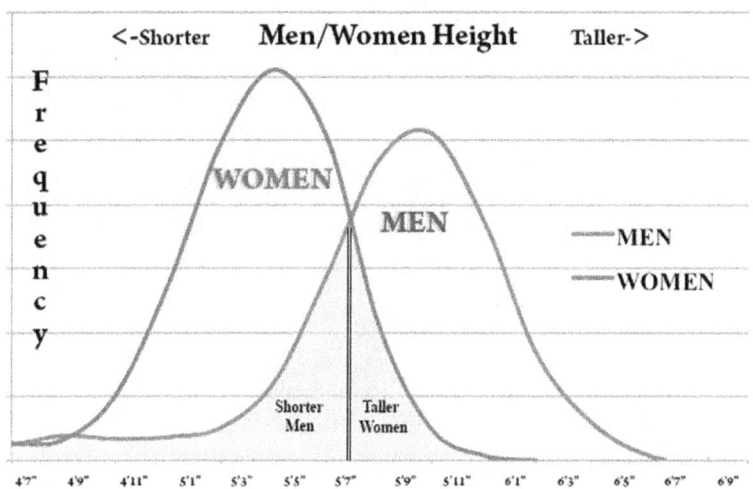

What we see on the chart is that the majority of boys are taller and the tallest are nearly always the boys. But you can also see that there are some very tall girls. Some of these tall girls are taller than many boys, but they are in the minority. What the chart shows is that most boys are taller than most girls but there

Helping Mothers Be Closer to Their Sons

are always exceptions. The same sorts of limitations apply to our discussions about our different brains or masculine and feminine traits. The world is not a black and white place. There are always exceptions and outliers.

The chart also shows us something else. It shows us that when you go to the edges of the data the split becomes more perceptible. When you look at people who are above 6'2" you find that it is almost all boys. By looking at the tails of the distributions you can learn things.

This turning towards the extremes of the distribution has been one of the ways that scientists have gotten more understanding about this testosterone flood. One example of a group that has been studied extensively is a group of girls who have Congenital Adrenal Hyperplasia (CAH). Girls with this disorder get high amounts of testosterone in utero, not unlike what the boys get, and guess what? They are more likely to want to play with "boy" toys, are more competitive, are more aggressive, have less interest in infants, less interest in nurturing behaviors, take more risks, and tend to enjoy competitive sports[5]. In many ways these girls are more like the majority of boys. The link is their similar testosterone levels in utero. The differences, attributed at least in part to the testosterone in utero, persist throughout the girl's lifetime. The organizational impact of prenatal testosterone has changed these girls for life. This flood of testosterone changes us whether male or female.

When you consider the CAH girls and the information we now have on boys' and girls' differences related to their levels of testosterone it becomes fairly certain that our prenatal testosterone levels are involved in our differences. Scientists have known for years that when you inject testosterone into a

It Starts Early

female rat in utero she will be born looking and acting more like a male.[9] There have been numerous studies on animals that agree that testosterone in utero changes their brains and their behavior later in life. We of course can't use the same intrusive studies on our boys and girls but having the information from these previous studies helps us in choosing where to look with humans.

Scientists agree that in utero testosterone seems to be linked to some of the differences we have discussed. This does not mean that these traits are due completely to our biology. Not at all. We are a wonderful blend of our brain differences, our hormones, our socialization, and our genetics. There is growing evidence that the SRY gene on the male Y chromosome is also involved in these differences.[10] They know that this gene signals the creation of the male's testes but have recently found strong evidence that it is also involved in the sorts of masculinization that we are discussing. These four, genetics, socialization, in utero testosterone, and hormones interact in a complex dance to bring us to our unique way of being and doing in the world. It turns out that some socialization can stimulate hormones, some hormones can turn genes on or off, and genes play a role in our hormones and behavior. It's a very complex interplay and I think we are just at the early stages of understanding. The important thing to note here is that biology does play a role. We have spent 50 years hearing that we are all blank slates at birth and all of our differences are due only to socialization. This view is incorrect and has caused considerable damage. Too often I have seen parents run under the assumption that since all behavior differences are socialized that the boys should be able to be taught to sit still and talk about their feelings just like the girls do. Those rascal boys just have to *want to learn,* and parents ask in frustration, "Why won't they learn?" We now know that *most* boys are likely wired in a way that will diminish their interest in learning to sit still and talk about their feelings. Their nature runs in a different direction. This is not to say they can't learn, just that their nature runs in a different direction and needs to be honored. We wouldn't complain to our red headed daughter that she should be able to learn how to be a blond. This does not mean we shouldn't work on helping our boys learn to sit still and have awareness of their emotions. It does say we need to love them for who they are and take their uniqueness into account when we expect them to learn behaviors that go against their grain.

We need to teach both boys and girls about their biological uniqueness and how they are different. After reading this book you will be in a better position to start that process with your own son.

It is also worth reiterating that while boys are better at systemizing this does not mean that girls are unable to do this. It simply means that the male brain is more built for that task. Conversely, because girls and women are more empathetic on average than boys this in no way means that boys cannot be empathetic. Just as our height graph showed, there can be very empathic boys and very system-oriented girls. All children are unique and it takes some loving and attentive investigating for us as parents to see our children's unique blends and strengths.

MALE-MALE COMPETITION

Have you ever noticed that your boys seem to want to win? Nearly all of the time? For many boys it is a very important aspect in their lives. They want to win, be on top, and be seen

It Starts Early

as a winner. Have you ever seen an argument between two boys about who won? I bet you have. My son would play his video game and not cease until he reached level 17. He was driven to get there. My daughter would play just to play and have fun. Why the difference?

Scientists are more and more convinced that these differences are related to testosterone. The pre-natal surge, the mini puberty shortly after birth and then the well-known testosterone increase during puberty are likely playing a part in this. With improvements in research techniques scientists are better able to observe testosterone in social situations and what they are finding helps us understand boys and men.

At one time testosterone was believed to be the root cause of aggression. Alan Alda started things off by claiming men were "testosterone poisoned" blaming men for their natural hormones and for the ills of the world. This silly and hurtful idea has sadly penetrated the public consciousness until now if you ask someone on the street what testosterone does they will likely say something about aggression or violence.

For many years scientists have tried to solidify a connection between testosterone and aggression but have come up pretty much empty handed when it comes to trying to connect activational testosterone with aggression. They knew that when someone was aggressive their testosterone would rise but what they now suspect is that it was the aggression that was raising the testosterone, not the other way around. In other words, for years it was thought that testosterone was instrumental in causing aggression but now they are thinking it is the aggression that is raising the testosterone. In fact this latest thinking on

Helping Mothers Be Closer to Their Sons

testosterone helps us greatly in understanding the role of testosterone in the lives of boys and men.

What the scientists are beginning to believe is that testosterone is more about striving for status and then maintaining that status. In the words of one expert, Christoph Eisenegger, testosterone "increases an individual's motivation and ability to acquire and defend social status."[11] This of course plays a large part in the social status hierarchies of boys and men. That is, who is on top who is second and who is last. It's easy to see how winning confers status and testosterone encourages us to win contests and strive for status.

But how does testosterone do this? Researchers have now confirmed that testosterone not only pushes boys and men to win it does so with a variety of help along the way. They now know that testosterone decreases fear and increases risk taking. It is much easier to strive for status and to win when our fear is diminished and we are more willing to take risks. The fearful person is more likely to sit on the sidelines. The one more likely to take risks is the one we would expect to jump in.

Another relatively new finding about testosterone is its tendency to increase what scientists are calling "threat vigilance."[11] By this they mean that testosterone pushes boys and men to be aware of anyone or anything that might be threatening their status and respond if necessary. In other words they are on guard against threats to their status. Have you noticed that? I bet you have but we just didn't have a name for it.

Another surprising element of testosterone is "Stress resilience."[11] Testosterone gives us a greater ability to bounce back and try again if we fail. You keep striving for status.

It Starts Early

Boys and men are built to strive for status and then to protect that status. Testosterone pushes them to win and to protect their winnings. It decreases their fear and encourages taking risks while it simultaneously gives them stress resilience.

But what is all of this striving about? Does it have any purpose?

Basically boys are in training to compete. Compete for what? Compete for mates. Yes, all of this wanting to be first and being focused on winning is connected to competing for mates. This of course is not in his awareness but it is in his hormones. This desire to win is directly related to his interest in striving for status that is related to his eventual striving for a mate and reproductive success. Boys compete for status and this status impacts where they fall on the hierarchy and this placement increases or decreases their chances of reproductive success since girls and women tend to be attracted to high status. Very attracted.

This is not just human boys, you can also see this clearly in the animal world. The Bowerbird is a great example. Male Bowerbirds build intricate and beautiful bowers to entice their potential females to choose them as mates. The females judge the bowers based on symmetry, color, and density. They also taste the male's paint. It seems that the males eat specific vegetation and combine that with their saliva to make paint that they use to paint parts of the bower. Apparently the female birds come and nibble on the paint as they inspect the bower and this plays into their choice of mate. The males work hard to build them and the females come and inspect the bowers and may the best bird win. The male Bowerbirds will do anything to win. They work for long periods on their bowers and have been known to visit other males' bowers and wreck them in order to increase their chances of success. The toughest male Bowerbirds are less likely to have their bowers attacked and this means that displaying toughness is a part of the male's potential success.

The young male Bowerbirds get a late start. In many animal populations and also in humans, the male's development is slower than the female. At birth an infant human female is about one month ahead of her male counterparts. By the time she is sixteen the difference is over a year.[12] Males in animal populations need the extra time to prepare for the rigors of male to male competition. In fact with Bowerbirds the males tend to hang out with adult males learning to build bowers until they are fully mature and start to build their own bowers. The females start reproducing when they are two years old but the male Bowerbirds don't even get adult plumage until they are seven

It Starts Early

years old and many don't start competing and building bowers of their own until they are ten.[13]

This Bowerbird example has some striking similarities to our human situation. The male Bowerbirds take longer to develop, their lives are built around competing and learning and practicing to compete and the female Bowerbirds do most of the choosing when it comes to mate selection.

Like the Bowerbirds our boys often focus on competing. But few of us connect our boys' competition with later reproductive success. There is no question that there is a connection, but in today's world people often will try to shame boys and men for competing, wanting to win, being first etc. Male to male competition in order to impress women has been an important force in the process of the development of the human race. It has been instrumental in building our culture. As men compete, things improve. Men's focus on competing and proving he is better than the next guy (in order to impress women) has been the fuel for men to compete and be the best to invent, to explore, to lead, to theorize, and much more. Male to male competition has produced a zillion better widgets and built many civilizations. It is what has pushed men to succeed.

It is interesting to note that it is the competition and the resulting hierarchies that have helped men to get along with each other. When men know their place on the hierarchy it makes it easier to cooperate. Just look at the military where the hierarchy is worn on your sleeve in the form of stripes. This overt hierarchy helps in knowing who is in charge and who is to do what. Men may not like this arrangement but they do respect it. Rank helps greatly in getting things done without extraneous arguments about who is better, who is in charge, etc. It seems that the male

Helping Mothers Be Closer to Their Sons

hierarchies that are developed out of male-male competition help men to know where they stand and this limits the fighting and disagreements that might otherwise occur. The office organizational chart serves a similar purpose. In some cultures that have less male-to-male competition and less clear male hierarchies, the murder rate can be considerably higher. The Gebusi tribe in New Guinea is one example where there is a void of male to male status striving and yet their murder rate is ten times what we find in some American cities.[14] Male to male competition may not be such a bad thing.

If our boys or our girls are interested in competing we need to love them for that and help them along the way. Trying to discourage them would be like mama Bowerbird telling her son not to try to learn to make bowers. It would go against his grain. It would be like the Big Horn Sheep mother telling her son to stop butting heads or the lion cubs to stop playing rough when young. If we did any of these things we would be thwarting their nature, their way of being. We need to be sure not to do that to our children.

Nature is often complex and a step ahead of us. The issue of competition and mate selection is no exception. Guess what? In some animal populations it is not the males that compete for a mate, it is the females! The two basic roles of competitors and choosers are not always what we might expect. In the seahorse and sandpiper worlds it is the female that competes to have the males choose her as the mate. Why? In those populations it is the males that spend more time raising the young. It seems that whichever sex is the one that spends more time raising their young will also be the sex that is the chooser. The other sex will compete for them and the child services they provide. The

It Starts Early

bottom line is that it is not your sex that makes a difference; it is whether you are a competitor or a chooser. In human populations it is primarily the males competing for the females and the females doing the choosing but there are plenty of times that females compete and males choose. It's not simple.

It is an interesting aside that biologists have found some important differences in both the competitors and the choosers whether male or female. The competitors are larger, more aggressive, more competitive, stronger, more violent and live shorter lives.[15] And yes, these qualities apply to the female sandpiper and seahorse as well as the many other male competitors. It's easy to see how this applies to humans and to boys in particular. Could it be that the shorter average male lifetime is related to males being in the competitor role? Most of the theories I have seen assume it is due to male tendencies toward risky behaviors. The bottom line is we are animals and though we have an advanced consciousness we also have our animal origins that still play out in our lives.

Daily Competing

So where do we see this competitive/hierarchical nature in boys as they grow? Just look in early grade school when the boys interact. Boys are very intent on words that end in "EST." Who is the fastEST, the tallEST, the strongEST, the funniEST. Boys are very sensitive to these superlatives and will remember for life the boys who are at the top. Just ask your closest male relative who was the tallest, toughest or fastest boy in his elementary school and see what he says. The boys are very aware of this arrangement: who is first, second, third, and where

Helping Mothers Be Closer to Their Sons

they fit in. They are also concerned about who is last and work hard to ensure it is not them. Just think of the way boys choose sides to start a game. Two boys pick. They pick the best boys first and then it goes down from there. I can remember being chosen near last and wanting so badly to be one of the first chosen, but that was not to be. My strengths were not the athletic type. But I learned an important lesson, as did the other boys when sides were chosen like this. We all learned exactly where we stood in the hierarchy. We knew who was first and who was second and who was last. Sometimes we would argue about these rankings. Sometimes with great passion. This data reinforced our ability to evaluate ourselves and told us just where our peers placed us. This was critical information and good practice for later work endeavors where we needed to evaluate our own skills and those of others.

As men age they continue their connection and sensitivities to hierarchies. What are men's favorite sections of the newspaper? Sports and business, right? What do those sections have in common? They are all about hierarchy. Who is on top and by how much. Think about those two sections of the newspaper. They are filled with hierarchical numbers. Every sports page shows the standings of the various teams. The standings are a blatant hierarchy. Who is on top, who is second and by how much. Oh, they are 4 games out of first place. Then there are all of the sports statistics, the quarterback ratings, rushing yards, batting averages, ERA's and so many others. Many boys and men understand this and love to discuss it in detail. Think hierarchy. And then there's the business section. Hierarchy after hierarchy. Just look at the stock market listings. The market is up today, the DOW is up 47, and on and on. Page after page of businesses daily ups and downs in the market. It's all about who

It Starts Early

is first, and who is last, and all points in between. This harmonizes with the male tendency towards hierarchy. Males live lives in hierarchies.

The boys experience this at play, where they want to win, at school where they want to be perceived as on top, and among their friends or siblings where they want to appear as high on the hierarchy as possible. Hierarchy impacts just about every aspect of a boy's life in some way.

What's that you say? Boys don't all want to be top at school? Correct. But look at each boy individually and you will likely see him striving for status in his own niche. This is what happens with males. They seek out their own niche and then strive for status within that niche. One young man might be striving to get a great GPA while another might strive more in athletic pursuits and another might strive to be the toughest. Another boy might strive to appear to not like school in order to be higher in his group's hierarchy. A college professor may strive for status based on how many articles he has published and in what prestigious journals. The football player strives for the NFL, while the musician looks for a hit single or playing in the best clubs. The criminal male may strive for the best crime while the monk may strive for enlightenment. It is a rare male who fails to strive for some sort of hierarchical success. It's an interesting fact that when males have a disease that drops their testosterone to near zero they cease wanting to compete.[16] This stuff is in our blood.

Helping Mothers Be Closer to Their Sons

DIFFERENCES IN WAYS OF GETTING WHAT YOU WANT

The sexes are different in their strategies to get what they want. This difference starts early. Boys tend to be more physical and direct, demanding or playfully pushing another boy in order to obtain what he wants. Girls don't seem to like this sort of method. Girls are more likely to use words or relational means to get what they want. Boys tend not to respond to this. Neither sex seems to be too keen on the other's modes.

To get a better idea of how boys and girls differ in this way, lets look briefly at the anthropological research of Ritch Savin Williams observing an adolescent summer camp.[17] Groups of boys and girls aged eleven to fourteen were housed in their own cabins. Let's look at the boys' cabins first.

Very soon after arrival, the boys started challenging each other, sometimes telling each other what to do, sometimes putting the other boys down. Each of these were maneuvers to try to attain higher dominance in the hierarchy of boys. Pushing and shoving was not unusual nor was making fun of weakness. In fact if weakness was exposed, the other boys would sometimes join in to mark their own dominance. Some boys barked orders and others followed, while some put up a challenge. The boys' pecking order, their hierarchy, was being made clear to all and it happened fairly quickly.

Savin Williams found that both boys and girls used ridicule and name-calling as a means to create higher dominance. But there were some strategies used by the girls that were very different.

Unlike the boys, Savin Williams says that the girls maintained a sweet and agreeable attitude for the first week, making friends

It Starts Early

and being nice. But after the first week was up the girls started their own ploys to gain dominance. Their modes were more relational and less direct. Girls would ignore someone, or appear to "not hear" another girl in order to maintain dominance. Other tactics included gossip, social alienation, misinformation and withholding eye contact.

The boys' strategy seems to be overt and out in the open. They seem to lack concern for the feeling reactions of their friends and are more likely to throw their weight around with bravado in order to be higher on the hierarchy. They just don't seem to care as much if someone gets hurt in the process. The important thing is to be on top. We can see this sort of thing when boys are together with their friends and they will openly put each other down. Moms get upset with this but it needs to be understood as being their way to navigate the hierarchy. This does not mean that we shouldn't help boys find kindness towards their friends; it does however mean that we need to understand these behaviors in their context.

The girls' strategy seems more passive and clandestine. Savant Williams tells us that the girls, unlike the boys, seem to want to be perceived as "nice" and maintain that image whenever possible thus they take a week to build alliances prior to starting to use dominance tactics. Their dominance strategies are designed to be stealthy. Their strategies are often easily denied as not being "on purpose" or by claiming they had no motive to hurt. All the while the hurtful behaviors flow via social alienation, gossip, exclusion and other means.

Both boys' and girls' strategies leave some chaos in their aftermath, the boys' more overt and the girls' more covert. Both strategies are designed to create and maintain dominance over their peers. It is easy to see how these very different strategies don't mix very well. This may play into what we will look at next, the very different ways that boys and girls choose to play.

PLAY

This stark difference in the ways that boys and girls work to get what they want may be a part of the reason that boys and girls have such different play patterns. Boys' and girls' play is markedly different and the difference starts fairly early. By the time boys are three years old they prefer to play with boys. This tendency to play with ones own sex increases through childhood. One study found that four-five year olds played on average three hours a day with their same sex peers and only one hour's time with mixed sex groups. Then when the children reached ages seven or eight the ratio of same sex to mixed sex groups increased to eleven to one.[18] Clearly the boys wanted to play with boys and the girls wanted to play with the girls. This pattern has been noted around the world in places as diverse as India, Japan, Canada, Kenya, the Philippines, Mexico and the U.S.[19]

Boys and girls not only differ in preferring same sex play, they also differ in the types of personal relationships they form both at play and in their leisure. The boys move towards a larger number of friends often forming coalitions while the girls tend to be more likely to form relationships with a single friend or maybe two. Let's look at the girls first.

Girls form relationships that are based on personal disclosure that offer high levels of intimacy and emotional support. They

It Starts Early

are often built as an intimate relationship that also serves well as a means of support in times of personal difficulties. The time commitment for such relationships is high as is the social risks of such personal exposure if the relationships fail as girls may become acutely vulnerable to relational aggression, ostracism and gossip. The time involved in maintaining such relationships tends to limit them in number.

The boys are different. Boys tend to form relationships with those in a coalition. In others words, being a part of a team. Personal disclosure is not mandatory. Specialization within that coalition is. When you are on the baseball team if you can play catcher that might be a valued asset within the coalition. Boys learn to work at having a specialty that is valued by their coalition. They also learn to be tolerant of other boys they might not usually want to be around if those boys are helping their team to win. Boys learn where their hierarchical place is within that coalition and strive to improve and they also get some gratification by being a part of the collective whole.

Evolutionary psychologists suggest that play in the animal kingdom is usually practice for what the animals will be challenged to do as adults. The young garfish play by jumping over sea turtles in the water. These skills are later used in escaping from predators. Lion cubs tend to pounce and to bat each other around in a rough manner, which also gives them practice at the later skills they will need as predators. Humans also seem to follow these same patterns. The two play patterns that are the most statistically significant are those of play parenting and rough and tumble play. As you can guess, the girls are far more likely to engage in play parenting in childhood and the boys are also more likely to engage in rough and tumble sorts of play which we see developing in boys (and some girls) by the age of three. Evolutionary psychologists suggest that these tendencies point towards the likelihood that boys may be rough later in life and the girls will be more likely to take on active parenting roles. Remember evolution does not care about what has happened in the last 50 years. It simply responds to what has happened over the last thousands of years and during those times the men were needed to protect the boundaries and the women were needed to nurture the young. This has left our boys with an urge to get rough.

In cultures that need to have the men protect borders from attack, the games they encourage young boys to play will often include physical combat. An example is the Sioux tribe in North America. One of the games the boys would play is the Swing Kicking Game. This game lined the boys up in a row facing each other. The game begins when the question is uttered "Shall we grab them by the hair and knee them in the face until they bleed?" At that point the boys started swinging and kicking with the object of getting their opponent on the ground and then kneeing them in the face. The boys who took a knee to the face would continue fighting bloodied or not. After the game, according to one report, the boys would laugh and talk about it with few ever getting angry.[20] These same skills would be later used by the boys when they would need to protect their tribe's boundaries and fight off intruders as a coalition. This sort of practice along with knowing their own strengths and weaknesses and those of their compatriots on their team would help them later in a real battle. Their play was preparing them for later danger. In cultures that do not need to have the men guard perimeters, boys are discouraged from rough and tumble, violent games. Interestingly, boys seem to gravitate and find ways to

It Starts Early

take part in rough and tumble play even if their culture discourages it. Having rough males who can protect your borders has been a very positive thing for cultures to have. Without it, many cultures would likely have died off.

The male capacity to protect has a number of benefits in keeping cultures alive and the inhabitants safe but it also has some significant drawbacks. The number of male to male murders that take place are about thirty to forty times the number of female to female murders that occur.[21] These male on male murders are usually not related to other crimes, but to disputes over status or a girlfriend. Again, it is hierarchy and competition setting off disputes that can be lethal. They usually occur in males who are fifteen to twenty-five years old and are more likely to occur if the male is unmarried.[22] Think dominance hierarchy and status. When a young man's status is questioned it can lead to great trauma especially if he is limited in maturity, under the influence of drugs or alcohol or mentally ill. The vast majority of men are able to contain this power without being inappropriately violent. A few cannot.

PRECARIOUS MANHOOD

We have seen how boys are impacted from within by their brain differences and organizational testosterone. We have seen how the testosterone pushes them towards competition, which then translates to impressing women with higher status and then to reproductive success. But there is another factor that greatly impacts boys not from within but from outside. Researchers are calling it "Precarious Manhood."

Helping Mothers Be Closer to Their Sons

When girls successfully go through puberty they are nearly always considered to be women. They have no need to prove their "womanhood" to anyone. It is simply accepted. Not so with boys. Boys may successfully navigate the physical side of puberty but this does not make them men. Manhood is something that he must prove. Repeatedly. Scientists have dubbed this phenomena "Precarious Manhood" and state that manhood is not a condition that comes about through biological maturation, rather, according to David Gilmore, it is a "precarious or artificial state that boys must win against powerful odds."[23] They have studied this around the world and say that this is nearly universal. In a wide range of cultures a boy often faces a difficult task to prove his manhood and even when he succeeds he must continue to prove his manhood throughout his life.

Generally at puberty and beyond boys are expected to prove their worth. According to a leading expert on this topic, Joseph Vandello, "manhood must be earned and maintained through publicly verifiable actions."[24] This unwritten mandate leaves men and boys anxious about proving themselves. Vandello's research has shown that men are indeed more anxious over this than are women and that in response to being challenged are likely to exhibit risky or maladaptive behaviors.

Whether it is on the soccer field, at school, with girls, or in schoolyard brawls, a boy's manhood is being observed and graded. This, along with his biology, creates a profound difference in a boy's life. His sister does not have the testosterone differences we have described; she is not pushed into a competitive mode, and is not graded at every step in a similar manner.

It Starts Early

These three things, testosterone, being the competing sex, and precarious manhood play a large role in how boys will act in the world, how they will behave towards themselves and others, and how others will perceive them. The testosterone pushes the boys to succeed from within as it pushes him to strive for status while the precarious manhood pushes him to succeed from outside as the culture demands he repeatedly prove his manhood. All the while he lives in an invisible hierarchical competing role that says he should win or at least look good in order to succeed reproductively. He gets it from all sides.

Knowing these things makes it easier to get a sense of boys and to understand some of their ways. Boys are thrust onto a stage that expects them to strive for status, to succeed, and to prove their worthiness at every step.

What does a boy need to do to win in this sort of scenario? One ironic answer is that he needs to do the very things that his parents have been telling him for eons but therapists have been telling him he should ignore. Things like be tough, be strong, big boys don't cry, and so many others. These messages begin to make more sense when you can see that the boy's parents love him and want him to succeed. They can intuitively understand that being tough and strong will place him higher on the hierarchy while crying will send him in a downward spiral. My sense is that parents are aware on some level that their son is indeed in a race and needs to look good in order to succeed.

The mental health industry has missed these critical differences and continues to push boys to be more like girls. One well known psychologist told me once that men simply need to developmentally "catch up" with women and that the world would be a better place if only men could be more like women!

Helping Mothers Be Closer to Their Sons

I hope you can see now the danger in that sort of thinking. All of the related urgings of the mental health professionals for boys like "you don't need to be tough," "be sensitive," "talk about your feelings," and "crying in public is a good thing," all go against the grain of the boy's nature. Knowing what we know now about boys and the world they face makes this sort of message counter productive in a world where he knows he needs to be tough to succeed. Being sensitive and crying in public would drop him in the hierarchy and make his task all the more difficult. With our boys we need to be aware of the stressors they face and help them navigate those as best we can.

This reminds me of an experience I had once when talking with a group of male psychologists. They were all impressed that the winner of the Heisman trophy had cried during his speech and heralded that event as a sign that things are changing and men and boys are becoming more sensitive. I had to chuckle. What they didn't understand was that when any man or boy is at the top of the hierarchy he can do whatever he wants. If he wants to cry he can get away with it since he is at the top. He is the proclaimed winner. Just think of what reaction they might have had if one of the runners up might have cried during his speech. They might have liked it but the world would see him immediately as a whiner and a poor loser.

We've gone over some of the basic male tendencies. The impact of the testosterone flood, the hierarchical mindset, the push to strive for status and compete, some information on boys and girls different ways of communicating and of getting what they want and their differences at play and lastly the impact of precarious manhood. With that under our belt we are in a good position to tackle something that has confounded women for

It Starts Early

some time: Why can't you see boys' and men's emotions? It's a story of how boys have creatively adjusted to the constraints of hierarchy, testosterone and precarious manhood. It's also a story that is very helpful for women to know in order to increase closeness with their sons.

Getting Close to Boys - Where are His Feelings?

Boys do indeed have emotions, you just don't see them as readily as most girls. Researchers were shocked when they did a study on the emotional reactions to teen relationship breakups. What they expected was the girls would be much more upset than the boys but what they found was that the boys actually had as much and sometimes more emotional pain after the breakup.[25] We know the boys have this experience but we also know that you usually can't see it. Let's spend a little bit of time looking at the reasons why it is invisible and this may help us to understand boys. When we understand them we are in a much better position to get closer to them.

Boys and girls have powerful emotions at birth, as infants and then as very young children. I think we would be hard pressed to claim there were significant emotional differences between them. However, as boys grow, their emotions seem to disappear. Most theorists maintain the idea that the boys are slowly taking on the masculine role socialized by our culture but I think we can now draw on our prior discussion to understand some of this from a different perspective.

The first element that keeps that emotional pain under wraps is the previously discussed male hierarchy and competitiveness. The older a boy gets the more he is impacted by these two

Helping Mothers Be Closer to Their Sons

elements. Once he reaches puberty, he starts to get the full dose of testosterone, which includes a push for him to avoid situations that might threaten his status (threat vigilance) and this shifts him into an even greater focus on hierarchy and competition. But why would hierarchy be involved in the invisibility of his emotions? Well, when you are in a hierarchy you strive to go as high as you can and avoid anything that might make you appear lower. Open emoting makes you go lower on the hierarchy. Lots lower. Why? This is because the hierarchy is based partially on independence. The more independent you are the higher you will place. Dependency is the bane of the hierarchy. Expressing emotions, except possibly anger, which may give the appearance of independence, will usually put you into a dependent position. Being hurt and sad, or being anxious are signs that you are not controlling your destiny independently. Boys will avoid this in order to appear to be independent and have things covered. Being in control gives you higher ranking in the hierarchy.

This practice of appearing to be independent prepares the boys for their later trial as men when they are disallowed to show any signs of dependency. For men to have high status they need to be independent and showing signs of dependency will actually bring the judgment from most in the culture that they are not "real" men. This is, of course, a manifestation of "precarious manhood." Author Peter Marin, an expert on homelessness, described this specific problem in an article where he wrote that the moment men say they need help they are judged as not deserving it:

To put it simply: men are neither supposed nor allowed to be dependent. They are expected to take care of others and

Getting Close to Boys – Where are His Feelings

themselves. And when they cannot or will not do it, then the assumption at the heart of the culture is that they are somehow less than men and therefore unworthy of help. An irony asserts itself: by being in need of help, men forfeit the right to it.[26]

Exactly! This is the plight of men, young men and to a lesser extent young boys. They are aware that any sign of dependency will negatively impact their image to women and other men and this leaves them wanting to appear independent. You can see this in young boys wanting mom to think of them as independent. Putting their best foot forward for boys is to appear independent, trying to stay as far up in the hierarchy as possible.

MALE PAIN IS IGNORED

Boys will avoid public tears if they can. A part of this is due to our culture being less interested in their tears than in their sister's. Most people are unaware of this difference but in our culture a crying woman is a call to action while a crying man means trouble to be avoided. I know this is hard to believe so let's try the following exercise in order to give you a sense of your own response.

Imagine you are being seated at your favorite restaurant. As you are walking toward your table you see a woman at a corner table crying with her head in her hands. What is your first reaction? I have asked this question to thousands of people in the workshops I give. The most frequent responses are "she's upset," "poor dear," and "she needs support." Think of what your own response was. Think too of your raw gut reaction to seeing this woman crying. Now erase that image and start a new

Helping Mothers Be Closer to Their Sons

image. You are walking into the same restaurant and as you are being seated you see a man at the same corner table that is crying. What is your first reaction? Most people respond that they are very leery of him: "there's something wrong with that man," or "he must be drunk," or other phrases conveying the sense that this man needs to be avoided. How about you? What was your response to the crying man? What was your gut reaction? Was there a difference in your reaction to the man and the woman?

When I first started using this exercise I was shocked to find that I too was more interested in helping the crying woman and avoiding the crying man! And I was working with men who needed compassion. This helped me realize that this response seems to be a part of our nature. Much has been written about boys and men and their reluctance to emote publicly but very little has been written about the stone wall the men and boys usually face if they do emote. Simply put, people are not interested in hearing the emotional pain of boys and men once the boys reach puberty. Very young boys are seen as cute and deserving of compassion but as the boys get older this willingness to offer them a loving hand becomes less and less.

You may wonder why it is that you and I both have an easier time in accepting the emotional pain of women? Why would a man's pain be taboo while a woman's pain would be a call to action? All of the hierarchical and competitive elements we have discussed with men are related to men's primary role of provide and protect. This role has meant that men have been expected to endanger their lives for thousands of years in order to maintain our culture. Every successful culture has made their males disposable in order to insure the protections and safety of

Getting Close to Boys – Where are His Feelings

women and children. This was a necessity. Those cultures that did not protect their women died quick deaths. Appearing tough and maintaining their role as protector has been important for men but women too are attached to the idea of men's invulnerability. It will take some time for both men and women to let this one go since it is connected to our survival instinct.

So there are at least two factors working here. Boys are working to strive for status and move as far up in the hierarchy as they can and will tend to avoid anything that might ruin their hard work. At the same time the boys, as they age, face an increasing indifference to their emotional pain and this adds to their reluctance. Now tell me, if you were to find that people lacked compassion for your pain would you want to broadcast it publically? I would bet not. Men and boys are not naive enough do that. We need to acknowledge that safe places for them are few and far between. Mom, keep in mind that you may be alone in your compassion for your older son. You and your family may be all he's got.

SOCIALIZATION

In addition to the factors discussed above, boys are socialized not to cry via precarious manhood. Boys face a very different world then their sisters. We are all aware of the socialization that goes on even today that encourages boys to be a certain way. William Pollack did a great job of laying out the many ways we socialize our boys in his best selling book Real Boys. Be tough, be strong, don't cry, never hit a girl and so on. Girls simply do not get a similar message. Girls also don't get the following dynamic: the first separation from mother. At about

Helping Mothers Be Closer to Their Sons

2-4 years old the boy goes up to mom and puts his hand on her breast just as he has been doing for as long as he can remember. But this time she takes his hand off and tells him not to do that. The boy is dumbstruck. Mom says "You can't touch me there." And he says back "But Suzie touches you there." Mom says, "Suzie's a girl." This doesn't make sense to him. Simply because he is a boy he has been denied access to his mother. He finds he can't take baths with mom or even be in the bathroom with her. He can't do the stuff he has previously done to get close to mom. He is cut off and ostracized. This is a confusing time. He is now more alone and has to find new ways to get close. Most boys are disoriented by this but in time start developing skills to be close to mom. He likely says to himself, "If I can't be close by touching I will try something else." So he starts a new strategy that centers on working to impress her somehow or even to protect her. He learns to come and go from mom and he learns to be more detached. In some ways this is the beginning of his striving for status that will be seen more clearly as he gets older. He seeks to impress mom in hopes of being close and being accepted and feeling like he belongs. It is these very behaviors that come into play later in his life when he strives to impress his girlfriend, and later his wife. By impressing her he is repeating his old strategy and is increasing his chances of closeness and, of course, his reproductive success.

This is also the beginnings of the provide and protect role the boy will be taking on as he ages. This role is an emotional straight jacket for boys and men. It forces the expectation that they will take care of others and be responsible and independent in the process of facing possible danger. It is on them to keep things running and safe and asking for help is discouraged. The more they can do it on their own the better they look in the hierarchy. But think about it. If you are expected to provide and protect others who is mandated to take care of you? No one. Once you leave mom, nobody. There is no third sex that is responsible to care for men and this leaves men knowing that they had better do it themselves pushing them farther into the independent stance.

So there are multiple factors influencing boys and men's emotions being invisible. Let's list them:

• Open emoting lowers his status in the hierarchy.
• Our culture has a distaste for the emotional pain of males.
• Our culture discourages dependency in males.
• The provide and protect role pushes protecting and providing for others but leaves no one to do the same for boys and men.

BIOLOGY AND EMOTIONS

There is one more important factor that keeps the emotional pain of boys and men unseen: our biology. The brain differences of systemizing versus empathy play a role. The brain that chooses to focus on systems is less likely to want to focus on emotional material than a brain that focuses on relationship and empathy. Perhaps more important is the testosterone differences. It turns out that testosterone limits ones emotional tears.[27] Boys after the age of twelve will likely experience a drying up of their tears as their testosterone increases. I know when I was a little guy I could cry with the best of them up until my twelfth birthday when the testosterone hit. I always thought I was just trying to be a tough guy but it is clear now that testosterone limits emotional tears. These young men will have the same emotional pain but not have the tears to shed. This is an important point. Imagine having a flood of emotional pain but being unable to use tears to release it. This is the plight of our young men. It's also interesting to note that males have larger tear ducts. Many are thinking that these larger ducts are instrumental in our seeing a lack of male tears. Ever notice that teen boys and men's eyes glisten with tears when they are very sad but the tears often don't roll down their faces like they do for many women? Some are thinking that the larger tear ducts are holding those excess tears.

There has been some research done comparing men and women and their expression and experience of emotions. Some of the data points towards the idea that women seem to experience a stronger inner sensation from emotions than men but results have not been conclusive. One meta-analysis of brain imaging studies showed that there was not a great difference in brain activation in men and women as they processed emotional material but did show that there were differences in the patterns of activation. Men seem to focus more on "the sensory aspects of emotional stimuli and tend to process them in terms of implications for required actions," while the women, however, "direct more attention to the feeling state engendered by the emotional stimuli."[28] This seems to suggest that men look towards emotions as indicators for what they need to do while women look at emotions as an experience and not an indicator of their next action.

When examining the testosterone research it becomes clear that very little work has been done on the connection of men's emotions and their testosterone. We are left with many questions about the connection of testosterone with our

Getting Close to Boys – Where are His Feelings

emotional states. One interesting study showed that when women were given testosterone their cognitive empathy dropped.[29] Another showed that when in a bargaining position that those given testosterone were more fair than those who were not given testosterone.[30] We have much to learn about this.

TRANSMEN

There is however, another avenue that can help us get a glimpse of these connections, the transmen. Transmen are biological women who sense they are male and proceed to take initiative to actually become male. This often involves biological women taking huge doses of testosterone. Many of the transmen have written on the experience of transitioning from female to male and the impact of taking very large doses of testosterone, large enough for them to grow beards, harden their skin, and a host of other masculine qualities. One transman named Max Valerio wrote an excellent book about his transition titled *The Testosterone Files*.[31] Max's writing eloquently describes some of the ways his emotional system changed with the introduction of large amounts of testosterone:

Slowly I began to realize that if I had felt this way as female I would have cried easily, released this pent up sadness and frustration through tears. Now I can't. I find it impossible to weep.

Max is clear that the testosterone stopped up his ability to cry. Max goes on to say:

On estrogen I was more relaxed, now I can hardly sit still. I

Helping Mothers Be Closer to Their Sons

find myself more confident, expansive and cocky. Now I understand teenage boys. Everything has a sexual sub-text.

I can remember working with women in therapy who had life threatening illnesses and had to take testosterone as a part of their medical treatment. They all said something very similar, something like: "Tom, I gotta get off of this stuff, I am irritable as hell and I can't stop thinking about sex." What I didn't say at the time but thought jokingly to myself was "Welcome to my world." I think many men might have a similar reaction. Max goes on to expound on this and tell us something very important:

I have noticed that when I am emotional it is more difficult to put my feelings into words. This is where women have a distinct advantage. I find it very hard now to explain or articulate my feelings when I am actually in the throes of feeling them.

Max is describing a very typical male pattern, one that I can testify as being accurate, that with testosterone, he found it difficult to articulate his feelings as he was feeling them. Every man I have talked to about this nods in agreement but the women are shocked. It is simply not a part of their world. They have usually assumed that everyone has the same ability to process emotions and this is incorrect. I have seen many women in couples therapy who are furious with their husband for his lack of articulation of his emotions. She assumes he is like her. I think it is clear now that he is not.

Max ends with the following powerful statement:

I had believed that men could cry just as much as women if they would just let themselves go. Men were victims of a masculine

Getting Close to Boys – Where are His Feelings

ethos that forbade tears that made them into unfeeling seething septic tanks of repressed pain ready to lash out. I was wrong.

Max sees now that his judgment of boys and men was a great error. He sees that living in a male body is a very different emotional experience. He now has a new compassion for men and boys and the way they work with their emotions.

I am betting that future research will validate what Max has described. Until then we will need to make our best guess, although new research is making some important inroads. The Affective Neuroscientist Jaak Panksepp has been mapping out the brain and emotions. Panksepp has found that the human brain has seven emotional systems and important for our purposes Panksepp has discovered that males and females are different in six of the seven systems.[32] We are different emotionally.

Getting Close to Boys - How Does He Heal?

We have discussed boys' unique paths, the sorts of pressures they are under and why it is difficult to see a boy's emotional pain. We can now turn to understanding how boys heal and this offers us an important pathway in getting close to them. Just imagine what it would be like for you if no one knew how you healed. If people basically ignored your unique needs. Would you feel isolated? Alone? Misunderstood? When we miss or misinterpret a boy's way of healing this pushes us farther away. When we know how he is healing it leaves us more in a place of understanding which gives us the opportunity for closeness even if we are not an active part of the process.

In order to understand his way of healing we will need to understand the basics of healing. What are the common strands that run through the different ways that people use to heal? This is what stumped me years ago when I was only thinking of healing as being about talking and open emoting. I wrongly assumed that if people were not talking about their problems and openly emoting they were not really healing. What I have since realized is that healing is first about finding safety. People don't heal when they are under attack, they are much more likely to heal when they have found a safe place. And there is great diversity in the safe places that different people find. What we want to guard against is the idea that "our" way is the "only" way. If we get stuck in that sort of thinking, like I was, we are in danger of not seeing the many ways that others might use.

The first element of healing then is finding a safe place. This helped me to start looking not for tears and emotions but instead to look first for where someone felt safe. It was pretty clear that many women and some men seemed to find safety in interaction with the people they loved. But boys didn't seem to feel as safe in interaction and neither did their dads. Their safety was different. Let's take a brief look at the research of Shelly Taylor of UCLA who helps explain this first and powerful difference between men and women and the ways they handle stress.[33]

Taylor found in 2003 that nearly all of the previous research on stress had been done using only male subjects. So what we know about the stress responses of "fight or flight" is likely true for men since they were the only ones studied. But what about women? Given this obvious bias, Taylor decided to find if women might have a different way from the standard "fight or flight" mode. Taylor set out to study only women and how they responded to stress. What she found was that when stressed women were unlike the men who usually fight or flight, they instead, will "tend and befriend." When stressed, women are more likely to move towards people and towards interaction. To care for and be cared for. Tend and befriend. This is a remarkable difference and provides the foundation for our understanding of how men and women, boys and girls might have different ways to process emotions and very different places to feel safe. Taylor helps us see that women will be more likely to move towards others and talk while men and boys will be less likely to do so.

Getting Close to Boys – How Does He Heal?

Taylor made an important discovery: she found that the hormone oxytocin was involved in these differences. Some call it the cuddle hormone since it often moves us towards affiliation, that is, it pushes us towards interaction and other people. Taylor found that both men and women under stress get an increase in their oxytocin levels. She was confused about why men and women would have such different strategies in dealing with stress but have a similar biology. What Taylor found was that women's estrogen tends to increase the affiliative nature of the oxytocin. When women get more oxytocin they *really* want to move towards others and cuddle. She also realized that the men's testosterone decreased the impact of the oxytocin. Men may get similar amounts of the hormone but testosterone minimizes the affiliative nature of oxytocin. Males didn't have the same urge to cuddle or move towards other people. This hormone obviously plays into men and women's different strategies of dealing with stress. We are often very different. Even in the basic ways we deal with stress and find safety.

Taylor's research tells us a couple of very important things. One, it tells us that women tend to feel safe in an interactive mode with others. Secondly, she tells us that men don't seem to follow the same pattern. Many men don't seem to find interaction and talking about their problems to be such a safe place. All the things we have discussed up to this point should help make that clear. Taylor does talk about fight and flight and as we will see these describe the men's path when stressed. Rather than go and tell someone about his problems he is more likely to want to seek safety in some action, or move to a safe place of inaction and ponder things. Fight and flight. It is worth noting that both of these modes insulate the men and boys from the judgments of precarious manhood.

But what happens once we find a safe place?

TELLING THE STORY

Once someone finds safety what is the next step? Think of what happens when most women, (likely you?) are stressed and find a close friend, you have a safe place and you have time to interact. What happens? It's obvious. You tell your story. There is something about telling the story that is healing and fulfilling. When you can get that story out and someone really hears it you feel differently. Often we feel affirmed and relieved. Safety and telling the story are the basic elements of healing that can be seen clearly in therapy or even a support group. Both therapy and support groups are built to help people to first feel safe and to then tell their stories within that safety. A therapist's office is built to help people find a sense of safety and the therapist works to reinforce that idea. As we find safety and tell that story our problems slowly become integrated into our being rather than something external that is hammering us from outside.

Safety and stories are the two elements that are basic to how people heal from very strong loss and trauma. It has been my experience that these elements are also used for everyday sorts of emotional bumps and bruises but on a smaller scale. The human mind is built to listen to and tell stories and this is for good reason. Doing this helps us stabilize and find our center. People find safety and then they tell their story within that safety. When I first started working with men I assumed that everyone felt safe sitting face to face and that everyone would benefit from verbally telling their story. I was wrong. It took me quite some time to realize that the basics of safety and story were the same for both men and women but the specifics of safe

Getting Close to Boys – How Does He Heal?

places chosen and the way the stories were told were very, very different. I began to realize that men and boys often found safety in their action (fight) or their inaction (flight) and then would use those modes to tell their story. It was right there for me to see but I missed it due to my assumption that everyone healed in the same manner.

This lays out our task. We need to first seek to understand where boys feel safe and then once we know that we can then start to determine ways they might tell their story. This is not an easy concept for those of us who are used to the interactive modes but it is critical that we learn to spot these in order to understand and have compassion for those we love that might have a different way of expressing themselves.

Having a look at these examples should make it easier for you to spot this in your own son, brother, husband, father, or any of the men you love. Let's start with a story…

When my daughter was little she would come to me and say "Daddy, I need special time." I knew just what that meant. She needed both a safe place and my attention. We would find two chairs that would face each other so we were face to face and she would proceed to tell me her stories. "Oh Daddy, Suzy said I was a dork." I would simply say, "Oh Julia" in a supportive tone. Then she would switch to another dilemma. "Daddy, Jenny said she would never play with me again." Again, I would offer her a supportive "Ah Julia." After about 5 or 6 "Ah Julia's" she would say, "Thanks, Dad." and run out the door to play some more. What was Julia doing? She was setting up a way to feel safe, to get my attention and then to tell her story as I listened. Very wise for a youngster and very effective. She

Helping Mothers Be Closer to Their Sons

knew how to get a safe place and then verbally process her story.

Did my son do that? Absolutely not. Luke had a very different strategy.

When Luke would come to me and say "I want to wrestle" I discovered that meant the same thing as Julia saying "Daddy, I need special time." I would tell Luke that he better be ready for me. He was just a little guy of maybe 6 or so and we would both posture and huff and puff and then the wrestling would commence. He would have me down and then I would have him down and back and forth it would go. At an unexpected moment he would raise his head up and say something like, "Jimmy got beat up today at school." I'd say "Was it bad?" And he would respond that Jimmy had blood on his shirt. Then back to the wrestling - as quickly as we had stopped we were back at it again. Then a moment later Luke raised his head and said, "I miss Granddaddy." My father had just died a few months back. My heart was touched and I responded that I missed him too. Then as fast as we stopped we were back to wrestling.

Can you see what Luke was doing? He was telling his story, a very intimate and sad story, in his own way and wrestling made it that much easier for him to tell it. It's important to note that there were many wrestling matches when he never opened up about something of great emotional import. It wasn't like wrestling was a feeling machine. It was just a time when it was easier for him to tell his story, a story that might be difficult to tell under other circumstances. By wrestling with Luke I was giving him that safety. He could then choose to use it or not. It was up to him.

Getting Close to Boys – How Does He Heal?

So our job is to keep our eyes open and see where our children or our loved ones find safety, a safety that allows them to open up and tell their story in their own way. Wrestling might not cross most people's minds as being a way to help our boys heal but it may be more common than most think.

I heard a story about a young boy whose mother died of an illness. He was 5 years old and went to attend grief counseling at one of the country's premier centers for children's grief, the Dougy Center in Portland Oregon. The young boy would attend the initial circle with his father and siblings and each visit he would then go directly to the Brio train table and play. He did this each time with the blessings of the staff. After a while he didn't play the entire time with the trains, he would take one of the trains and put it in his pocket and then do different things around the center. Some might wonder what this boy was doing and some might even suggest he was avoiding his pain since he wasn't talking about it. However, what the staff found out after a while was that the boy and his mother had a ritual each day to visit the train tracks very near their home and watch the afternoon train pass by. His play with the Brio trains was a safe place for him. It was a way for him to be with his mother. A safe way to remember their time together. This is telling the story. Can you see that as he was playing with the trains he was obviously thinking about his mom, being with his mom, remembering his mom? The trains were a safe place for him and his play helped him in remembering his mom and their times together.

This boy was using play as a means to help him tell his story and this is a very common strategy for children who are working to process their emotions. Careful observations of children and their ways to tell their story has led to play therapy as being a

Helping Mothers Be Closer to Their Sons

useful and popular therapeutic modality. Simply sitting with the child and playing with them allows them a safety and their story comes pouring out. What therapists have found is that by being with the child in the safety of their play, the story unfolds from the child often as a part of the play.

If you were this child's parent what could you do to be of help? I hope you can see that the best method is to enter into his safe place. In this case it would likely mean that you would play with him. Probably play with trains. Get a set of Brio trains and lay with him on the floor and play with him. If his mom came up as you are playing that would be great, if not, that is okay too. Just the act of playing and being with him is important. You might want to ask him if he would like for you to take him to see the afternoon train together. Then follow his lead. He may say no and that would be fine but he also might be excited and that trip could only help him process his emotions around the death of his mother. Find his safe place and be there with him shoulder to shoulder. Your loving presence is more important than the words that are spoken.

I was trained as a play therapist in the 1970's and can tell many powerful stories about simply being with children, playing with them and watching kids deal with trauma by using their play. Jimmy is a good example. He was 8 years old and from a family where he was physically abused by both parents. Jimmy and I would sit or lie on the floor of the playroom and play with action figures. He would tell stories about these figures and invariably his stories would have marked similarities to his own situation. Jimmy felt safe at play with these figures. As we played we talked about the action figures. What was this guy doing, and what it was like for the action figures to experience these things. He was open about this and enjoyed pondering

Getting Close to Boys – How Does He Heal?

what it was like for them and what could be done to help them. We could talk freely and openly about the action figures as we played on the floor in the room built for play therapy. I am guessing you can imagine how this worked and how over time Jimmy started working through some of his issues. Importantly, Jimmy really enjoyed the play and so did I. It's where he felt safe and I was able to be with him in that safety.

If you wanted to help Jimmy what would you do? Get some action figures and get on the floor and play. He obviously feels safe with the action figures and once he plays he will tell his story in his own way. All you need to do is play with him. Not directing or controlling, just being with him. He will thrive on having you play with him. He doesn't need you to talk or say anything, just play. It's a win/win.

I once worked with a young man whose girlfriend was killed in a car accident. The young man was distraught and crushed by her death. Shortly after the death he did connect with some friends and talk about her and how hard it was for him. As time went on he found he had a great deal of pain due to her death and he found some creative ways to work with it. He played guitar and he started to write songs about her. He didn't share any of this with many people. He kept it mostly to himself (invisible to most) but the songs were about her and about their time together and they were very emotionally powerful. Can you imagine as he is writing these songs what might be happening to him? He was surely experiencing the emotions surrounding her loss but he was doing so in a way that had nothing to do with talking and everything to do with an activity that helped him move into the feelings and slowly release them. No one told him to do this. No one instructed him about what to do. He did it on his own without any direction. This is a great example of a young man using his creative action to help him with his emotions. He was telling his story through his creativity and his emotions and reactions were likely similar to what you might expect from someone else attending a support group.

How could you be of help to this young man? Would you ask him to sit and talk about his feelings about the death of his girlfriend? No. How about asking him about his songs? Which is your favorite? What is the newest song? Can you play one for me? The young man would be more likely to want to share a song than to sit and talk face to face about his feelings. As he played you can imagine the emotions would pour out. By focusing on his music you are entering his safe place. If he allows you to enter all the better but also know that he may not really want to share this. That's ok too.

A young teen client came to me due to his upset surrounding his best friend's suicide. He found himself in the midst of the chaos and shock of not knowing what had caused his friend to end his life. A part of what this young man did to help himself was to study suicide. He read books on the topic and worked to understand what might have happened. In the process he became close with the father of his friend and the two spent time together working to make sense of this seemingly senseless act. This young man was very bright and was using his thinking action as a means to both understand his story and tell it. When the young man and the father would talk it is likely their conversations would include their pain and powerful emotions but the focus was not on feelings, it was on understanding. They offered each other support in a very masculine manner, by honoring each other's actions and both benefitted greatly.

Getting Close to Boys – How Does He Heal?

Can you see how an easy way to connect with this young man would be to ask him about what he has learned? Talk about his efforts and what might have surprised him or helped him to understand. Enter his safe place and let things happen. His emotions will simply be a part of the story that he tells.

Many parents have experienced the following scenario. Your teen son has just had a limit set. He is not happy and he goes to his room and slams the door behind him. The house shakes a bit. You are left wondering. Fifteen minutes later you hear nothing. Thirty minutes later you hear nothing. Then about an hour later he emerges from the room and asks what's for dinner. What has just happened? The young man was using "flight" as a means to heal. He likely went into his room and steamed a bit and told the story of what was happening to him over and over in his head. We call this "grinding." He was mentally grinding on the problem in his own mind. This is the inactive mode of healing. The story is told repeatedly and over time it slowly helps bring a bit of stability back to the boy's psyche.

What could you do for this young man? Plenty. Stay away and give him his space. He is telling you that he needs space and if you try to interrupt that you are literally foiling his safety. Give him his space and when he re-enters the world let him know he is cared for and valued.

This inactive mode is one that really bugs the more extroverted parents. But remember, it has been a healing agent for men for centuries. Great men and even religious leaders have found great solace and healing in solitude. Think of Jesus when he was in trouble. What would he do? He would seek solitude and head to the desert for 40 days and nights and I don't remember Mary following him in and telling him he needed to join a support group. No! She let him be and sometimes we need to let our boys and men be. Knowing when to let them be and when to interact is a real skill that we all can work on.

MICHAEL JORDAN AND PRACTICAL ACTION

We are all familiar with Michael Jordan. He is surely one of the greatest basketball players to ever play the game. Jordan's father was murdered in August of 1993. Two months later Jordan announced to the world that he was leaving basketball. In another two months he announced he was going to make a huge switch and play professional baseball. People were shocked and saddened that Jordan would leave basketball and the thought of him playing pro baseball was even harder to fathom. Why would he do such a thing? People were scratching their heads and many still don't know what was behind his switch.

Here's the rest of the story. What we now know is that Jordan's father, James, had always wanted Michael to be a professional baseball player. Before his death he had urged Jordan to drop basketball and move to baseball. Now just four months after his father's death Jordan was announcing that he would be playing pro baseball. Jordan was honoring his father with his action. Bob Greene quotes Jordan talking about his time in the minors in his book Rebound: "So on my drive to practice in the morning, he's with me, and I remember why I am doing this. I remember why I am here. I am here for him."[34] It's clear that the action of playing minor league baseball acted as a safe place for Jordan and more importantly was also a way to honor his father. Through honoring his father and his father's wishes he was remembering his father and telling his story while he also was forging a new story that honored his dad.

Getting Close to Boys – How Does He Heal?

Jordan also helps us see how the masculine path of honoring will often pull the man into the future. Jordan changed his future to honor his dad. By doing this he was basically saying, "I love and respect you, Dad." Obviously, Jordan's dad was with him in spirit as he practiced and played. His emotions were clearly a part of his honoring. The same emotions that someone else might experience in going to a therapist or a support group of some sort, Jordan was experiencing this through his practical action and his honoring.

Importantly most people had no idea that Jordan's switch was a part of his healing. Jordan's practical action helped him to connect with his loss just as the young man's songs about his girlfriend did but people generally never see it. It is stealth for the reasons we have already explained.

If you were Michael Jordan's friend how would you support him? Would you suggest he talk about his feelings for his father or would it be more productive to ask about his baseball efforts?

Let's take just a moment to observe the five types of healing action we have described. Play, creative action, thinking action, inaction and practical action. Notice that all of these actions don't negatively impact men in the hierarchy thus short-circuiting the judgments of precarious manhood. Note too that most of the actions are connected with a product like the young man's songs or Jordan's baseball career and therefore pushed him higher in the hierarchy and avoided harsh judgments related to his feeling states. It's easiest to start seeing these by observing what men and boys tend to do following a very strong loss. Here are some examples:

PLAY -- We have already seen two examples of play from

boys, one who played with action figures and the other with Brio trains. Children will often draw and paint what is bothering them; in fact there are a number of coloring books available for parents and children to color together with various themes. Coloring together gives the kids a safe place and the conversation that accompanies the coloring helps them tell their story.

CREATIVE ACTION – Many people use creative action to tell their story like the young man who wrote songs about his girlfriend. You can also see this creative action in adults who use actions like painting, singing, sculpting, writing music, listening to music, and a host of other creative paths to connect them with the things they find upsetting. How many symphonies have men written in honor of a loss? The AIDS quilt is a great example of telling the story through creativity. Each panel literally tells the story of one person who died from the disease. Seeing the entire quilt gives one a glimpse into the enormity of the emotional pain that is connected to this disease.

Getting Close to Boys – How Does He Heal?

THINKING ACTION – Some men study like the young man in our example studying suicide. Some journal, some study their loss, some dedicate their learning, some philosophize, some meditate, and others write articles or books. Each of these actions can help put him closer to his problems, his feelings, and to tell his story

INACTION – This is simply telling the story internally, in our own heads, by ourselves. Some will do this before going to sleep, others while driving, and some others while taking a walk. The young man in the example above simply went to his room. It can happen anyplace. You likely won't see it unless they tell you about it. They are probably telling this story over and over again in their heads. Like the other three types of action this one is basically invisible. You can't see it.

PRACTICAL ACTION - This is probably the most common path whereby men and young men and some young boys use practical action as a vehicle to tell their story. Like Michael Jordan, some men might dedicate their work, others might build a memorial or start a trust fund, still others might dedicate themselves to better parenting. I have seen boys promise they will do better at school or at home in honor of a serious loss. Think of the NFL when a player or owner on a team dies. What do these men do naturally and without direction? They honor their fallen comrade with an insignia or patch on their uniform and they dedicate their season (their action) in honor of the lost friend. Their play is now connected to their loss and the future becomes a way to remember this friend and to tell your story. But all of this happens through action, not just sitting in a circle and talking.

Helping Mothers Be Closer to Their Sons

It is this invisibility that kept me from seeing the way men and boys used action in order to heal. Men and boys, for many good reasons, are very good at making their healing paths invisible. It is likely that you are unaware of how he does this. I'm sure you can see now that these actions not only keep their pain invisible they also connect their healing with something that helps them to seem more independent and therefore doesn't drive down their standing in the hierarchy, doesn't ruin their competitive efforts, and doesn't set them up to be questioned by precarious manhood tests. Jordan's baseball, the young man's songs, the boy's trains, and the studies of the other young fellow, all of these were ways to process emotions quietly and invisibly.

Add to this that many of these healing paths had to do with the future and you can see the stark contrast with the traditional modes of healing which emphasize talking about the past and open emoting. To someone attached to the traditional ways of healing, action and a pull towards the future appears to be avoiding the pain when in fact it is the opposite.

By knowing your son's ways to find safety and then to listen to his story you will be in a much better position to be close. He will appreciate your understanding.

APPLYING THIS TO YOUR SON

Let's think for a minute about your own son and his ways of healing. Here are five ideas about possible thoughts and interactions you might have with him to try to learn more about his ways.

Getting Close to Boys – How Does He Heal?

On Your Own

1. Think of your son. Where do you think he finds safety? There are three basic places that people will find safety: Interaction, Action, and Inaction. Most of us will use all three of those but one will usually be primary and be more helpful than the other two. When he is stressed does he want to talk about things (Interaction)? Does he move towards doing something (Action)? Or does he isolate himself and get quiet (Inaction)? If he uses action does he move towards creative action, practical action or thinking action? Think of his unique way.

With Your Son

2. When things are calm and relaxed ask him something like "When you get upset, what helps you feel better?" Have fun with this question and if he responds humorously don't get too serious. He may say "Dessert!" If he does, ask him what kind and how many! He may say "Lots of money!" And ask him how much. Let the conversation go wherever it goes and learn from what is said. You can always come back to the basic question in a couple of days. Make it an informal and relaxed interchange if you can. Think play.

3. Another option might be to start by telling him what *you* do to feel safe and what you do to help yourself and then ask him if that sort of thing works for him. If he says no, then ask what does help him. It could prove to be a valuable conversation. Be sure to ask this in a place where he feels comfortable and listen very carefully to what he says.

4. When things are calm and relaxed, ask him what happens to him when he is upset, what's it like for him and would he rather talk about it, do something or go to his room and think about it. (This is assuming his room is a safe place for him). Listen carefully and ask open ended or clarifying questions.

5. Ask him when things are calm, when he is in the middle of being upset what is the best response from you? What could you do for him that would be most helpful? What are the things that might help when he gets upset? Boys are not accustomed to hearing this question. Give him time and tell him he can think about it for a while and you can talk more later. His responses can be very instructive in leading you to be helpful. Listen carefully and do your best to follow through. You might also ask about the things you do when he is upset that he finds irritating or unhelpful.

The point here is to start a conversation that may help you understand your son and his way of healing. Remember, he may not even know that he is using these safe places. This sort of safety seeking is done automatically and without direction. Be sure to make the conversation informal and relaxed unless he chooses to make it serious. Follow his lead.

Don't be surprised if he says he likes to just be by himself. This is often the response that boys will give and you already know from the previous chapter about why this will likely work better for him. He will probably not be aware of the ways he puts his emotional pain into action and will also likely tell you that he doesn't really want to talk about it. Then again, he may say just the opposite. This is where it is critical that you listen carefully and if you don't understand his responses just ask questions. If he says he doesn't want to talk about it anymore ask him when a

Getting Close to Boys – How Does He Heal?

good time to talk might be. If he says NEVER, tell him that you really care about him and want to learn from him how to best help him when he is feeling crummy. If he says leave me alone, ask him when or how you will know it is time to connect with him. Whatever you do, don't force him to talk if he doesn't want to.

If you feel it is important to initiate an interaction with him about something that is bothering him here's a suggestion that might be of help. Ask him "What is the toughest thing about this for you?" This question plays to his strength. First it acknowledges that he is dealing with something that is tough, second, it doesn't ask him what he is feeling, and third it approaches it from a hierarchical standpoint. Be ready for him to tell you the toughest thing for him. When he tells you this it is an easy path to simply ask him what it's like dealing with that tough thing. See how it works with your son.

Knowing your son's ways to heal can be a real door to closeness. Remember, talking is not always necessary. Acknowledging him and just being with him shoulder to shoulder is a real boon for him. There are plenty of other ways to get close to your boys and the next chapter we will be looking at some general ideas about how you can get close to your son.

Getting Close to Boys

We have learned about boys being influenced by their testosterone in utero, their connection to hierarchy, competing for mates and the outside push from precarious manhood. We have seen how this impacts the ways they choose to heal and have started to examine some of those ways to heal and how we can get close to them in the process. This section will take a more general look at how to get close to boys.

All children want to know they are cared for. That is a given. But with boys their unique qualities add on a different need. When you are in the midst of competition and hierarchy it is encouraging to hear you are succeeding. This is why messages that convey admiration or respect are fuel for your son. In fact, when a young man is admired one of his first responses is that he will relax and open up. Why? As we have already seen, boys live in a hierarchical world and when those they love admire them and think they are succeeding it gives them a break for having to impress and hold up their best face. I teach women in the workshops I give that if you want your husband to open up, admire him. Only do so if you are sincere. Men will pick up insincere admiration in a fraction of a second so only offer admiration if you truly feel that way. But once he is admired and he feels it is sincere he will likely tell you what he could have done better. It will be much easier for him to talk about his

Helping Mothers Be Closer to Their Sons

flaws once he feels he has succeeded. So you can keep in mind during this section that admiration and respect are fuel for the masculine and they don't cost a penny!

Let's start with a short story:

Imagine two men in a fishing boat. They spend the day quietly fishing with an occasional word about the weather, the catch, the bait, or the local sports team. When day is done, they feel close with each other after a shared activity that both enjoyed. They don't talk about it.

Now imagine if one of the men in the boat kept bringing up a topic that the other didn't really want to hear about. What would happen? It would sour the day and probably limit the amount of satisfaction and closeness at the end of the day.

Don't be that guy!

Participating with your son in a shared activity can be a time where you feel close, but if, like the above example, you try to push an unwanted agenda the time gets soured.

The theme to keep in mind is to "be" first, talk later. If you want to get close with your boys, find a way to be shoulder to shoulder and do things together. This is likely where they feel safe, and telling them what to do is not being shoulder to shoulder.

So what are the active modes that you can join together and be shoulder to shoulder? There are plenty. How about playing a game of catch with a football or throwing the Frisbee? The focus of the event is the Frisbee or the football. Just toss it back and forth and if a conversation pops up you take his lead. If not, then just enjoy the game of catch and the opportunity to do

Getting Close to Boys

something together. I am sure you have plenty of other ideas like taking a walk, a back rub, doing yard work together, or just about any other shoulder-to-shoulder activity. Any of these can be a safe place for a young boy. Keep your eyes peeled for your son's safe places.

It's not a bad idea to have a Koosh ball handy. In the winter when you can't go out to play catch, you can sit in the house and play catch with a little Koosh ball. You will be amazed at the topics that come up as you are simply tossing the ball back and forth. Do not bring up topics. Let him bring up whatever he wants and then respond. In fact the Koosh ball is great for you and your husband to use. Guess what? Your husband will enjoy tossing it back and forth and the darnedest things can come up as you are playing catch.

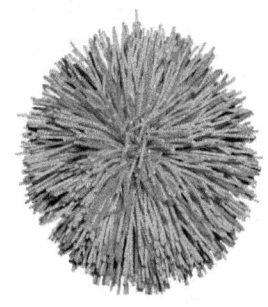

The same idea can be used when you need to have a conversation with your son and want to make it go a little bit easier. Get out the Koosh ball. The sitting still thing is not easy for boys and I have found it can help the flow of a conversation to have a simple Koosh ball to toss back and forth during the talk. Then again, use caution. Sometimes the ball can be used to avoid things. You be the judge.

Here's a possible scenario:

Tell him you need to talk and sit down in whatever room you will be using and bring the Koosh ball. Start tossing it back and forth. Get into a rhythm of tossing it and then as you are tossing

Helping Mothers Be Closer to Their Sons

it back and forth bring up your topic. Discuss the issue while you are tossing the ball. I think you will be surprised at how much easier the conversation flows when there is a simultaneous game of catch. I know this sounds a little nuts but give it a try and see how it works for you and your son. You are basically meeting him halfway by merging his way of feeling safe, the game of catch, with the needed interaction. I know many parents who have found this very helpful. You could just as easily go out and play catch or shoot baskets and talk while you are playing. This activity gives the boy a safe place while he is in the midst of interacting. It makes it a bit easier.

This little game of catch plays into the boy's need to move and his irritation with having to be throttled and held still. Even a small outlet like this can help satisfy that need and improve the quality of the interaction.

I know one mother who needed to have a serious conversation with her older son. She remembered she had a large container of coins that needed to be sorted. She asked him to help with the sorting and as they sorted she brought up the issues she had worried about discussing. The sorting and discussing were both a success. This mom found a way to incorporate a shared shoulder to shoulder activity with her needed discussion. This is a win/win. By giving him a safe place things went very smoothly.

Another tip for a conversation is to sit on your son's right. Research shows that men and boys take in more from their right ear than their left. Weird, eh? Hey, every little advantage can help.

We have seen how boys are often interested in competition and this is another way to be with them shoulder to shoulder. Learn

Getting Close to Boys

how to play HORSE. It's an age-old basketball game that boys know very well. Here are the basic rules. Person A takes a shot. If he makes it then person B has to match that shot. If B does not match it then he gets an "H". If A does not make his first shot then B gets to try and make one and if B makes the shot person A has to match. It goes back and forth until someone ends up with "HORSE" which amounts to having not been able to match the other person's shot five times. Try it with your son and see how it goes. My guess is that he will enjoy competing with you. He will likely enjoy beating you soundly even more.

Another topic that needs to be mentioned is video games. Boys generally love to be playing and striving to get to the next level. The world disappears and they become immersed in a new world. All too often his love for gaming can become a family struggle with the basic theme being that he is neglecting his schoolwork and just about every other thing in his life. So how can this be leveraged as a safe place? In an interesting way. Ask him to teach you his game. I have recommended this strategy to many parents and even more so to grandparents. They find that the boy is more than willing to help them learn the game and as he teaches, it gives him the experience of being the expert, of being the one who knows, the one who is listened to and asked for advice, the one who is in charge. This is often a new role for the boys and they love it. Think hierarchy. He is now on top and you are on the bottom. His skills are valued and sought after. When boys feel they are at the top of the hierarchy they are much more likely to open up about what might be bothering them. Even if they don't open up the experience for boys to be on top and have their opinion valued is a huge plus in his development. Additionally, when you learn more about his game you will be more able to find the best times for him to take a break. "But mom, I can't stop now, I am at the village gates…" and mom says "Ok, get to the first pilot and save the game then its dinner time."

It is worth noting that gaming is one of the last places in our culture the masculine exists in its raw form. Gaming is only concerned about winning, fierce competition, pushing and shoving verbally, forming a hierarchy and seeking ways to be on top. Being nice is not on the menu. Think back to the examples we offered about boys in the summer camp cabins. See the similarity? Also know that nearly every other avenue for masculinity has been stifled and replaced with being nice and getting along. It is no wonder why boys love gaming.

Another idea for younger boys is to build a fort. Take the couch cushions and prop them up to make an enclosed space. Get inside the fort with him. It is very likely he will like this experience but it does more then just having him like it. It gives him a space with you where he feels very safe and contained. Bring a little snack into the fort. You might even get him to tell you a little story about your fort, what are the walls made of? Who are the enemies and why? What are you and he doing there? Is he protecting you? Is he the Commander of the fort? Get him talking about his story and through his story you will learn all about what he is thinking and feeling. Listen carefully without judging. Just enjoy being together.

STORYTELLING

Storytelling is a great way to get close to all children but it is especially good for boys. Why? What happens to a child or even an adult when you tell them you are going to tell them a story? They immediately relax and go into a receptive mode.

Getting Close to Boys

They know they don't have to do anything, they are not being graded and can just sit back and listen. Think back to a time when you were young and someone told you they were going to tell you a story. Remember that feeling? No responsibility, no precarious manhood or competition or hierarchy, just waiting for a story.

I would urge you to get a copy of Grimm's Fairy Tales. Go for the original stories and avoid any revised politically correct versions that make them all nice, no, get as close to the originals as you can. Pick one story and read it on your own. You might want to choose one that is unfamiliar. One of my favorites that very few people have heard is titled "The Nose." It's earthy and boys love it, especially the expanding nose part. Read that one or one of your choosing several times and get a handle on how the story goes. When you feel ready tell your kids the story from memory. You might want to make a cheat sheet with 4-5 of the major plot turns just in case you forget. Yes, you might forget and leave some things out but it adds spontaneity to things that reading from a book misses. But not to worry, this is not for everyone and you may just want to read and that is much better than not telling it at all. If it is a fairly long story consider telling it in two parts. They love this. Well, they hate it when you stop but they will think about it the next day and look forward to it. When you start back the next night ask them where you left off and get a sense of how well they are listening. During the telling pick a place or two to stop and ask them, "What would you do if this was you?" Boys love this question and will tell you what they think is the best path for the protagonist and why. You will learn lots about him by listening. Listen to his ideas and then go back to the story.

Helping Mothers Be Closer to Their Sons

TELLING STORIES WHERE YOU MAKE THEM A PART

One of the things that young children love is if you tell stories that involve them as characters. This takes a bit of planning and creativity on your part but the payoff can be huge. The story can be whatever you would like it to be but for boys if there were an element of adventure and risk it will likely go over better. I would tell my kids what they named the "Ice Cream Story." They loved it and would never fail to want to hear it again. Each time I told it we would add something a little different but the framework would stay about the same. The ice cream story was about my children and sometimes their friends (depending on who was present) inadvertently finding a huge storehouse of ice cream that flowed from faucets and an even bigger supply of cones and toppings (sprinkles, gummy bears, etc.) in the cabinets above the sinks. They would feast on these only to be nearly found out and then find ways to make things right. The story ends with the idea that they would return to that treasured storehouse whenever they wished and live happily ever after. In telling the story each child would be incorporated into the tale, i.e. "Suzy found the trail that led to the mysterious faucets and Jack ran to the nearest one and turned it on and what do you think came out?" They all scream at once, "Ice cream!" What flavor ice cream came from your faucet? Each child plays a part in the adventure and you can choose their part based on their skills and personality. Then again, listen to them as the story is being told and go with their ideas about their part. If you listen they will let you know what they want their part to be. If you are a creative type you can just make it up as you go. It can be great fun and everyone has a good time. Remember, you are not being graded either. Just relax and have some fun. If you mess it up, all the merrier. Boys love a mess.

Getting Close to Boys

TELLING STORIES AS A GROUP

One fun thing to try is to have a group story. You will have to gauge if this will work for your situation but here is what happens. You get the story started and then each person takes turns adding what happens next in the story. It nearly always takes twists and turns and gets very humorous. It's just for fun but everyone usually enjoys the process. The hardest part is finding an ending. The boys usually give the story some pretty odd and earthy twists. Listen carefully, they will tell you a great deal in their plot twists.

STORIES FOR OLDER ADOLESCENTS

One last thing about storytelling. There are some stories that can be of help to your older sons when they are in their adolescence. The Trickster stories. They can be found in a book by Paul Radin titled "The Trickster." **Please read these stories first before you hand them over to your son.** They are very earthy and bawdy. More so than you are likely imagining right now. Young men love these stories if only for the absolute manic zaniness that Trickster takes part in on a regular basis. Just to give you an example, in one story Trickster takes his penis out of his pack on his back (yes, it is all explained in the stories) and sends it across the lake to have sex with the chief's daughter! Another of the tales has trickster nearly drown in a sea of his own poop. Issues of sexuality, morality, arrogance, and violence are common in the tales. They offer a great tool to foster discussion about these difficult issues. Read the stories together and see what comes up. Maybe have a Trickster tale told after dinner once a month? These are very powerful stories that are raw and in their original form from the Winnebago tribe

Helping Mothers Be Closer to Their Sons

of North America. Your sons will not forget them. They are also not for everyone.

LEARN FROM HIM ABOUT HIS SPORT

Another way to get close with your son is to learn all you can about the sport he is playing. If he is playing soccer learn the positions and especially his position. Learn the rules of the game and ask him questions about things. When you don't know about things get him to teach you. For instance get him to teach you about the nuances of the offside rule in soccer. I remember it took me a while to understand that one and my son enjoyed my ignorance and my finally getting it. Your son will love it if you are very interested in learning and this can lead to extensive technical discussions between the two of you about his games. This is guy talk, this is fun.

GO CAMPING

This is a win for boys. Getting out where they can run and be active is a big win for many boys. They may love to work to make the fire, put up the tent. Then again, not all boys might like this. Think of whether your boys would. Think of ways to challenge your boys. Who can be the first to find a red leaf? Who can gather the most firewood? Etc. Think hierarchy.

COMPETE WITH HIM

Challenge your son to a foot race. Set the rules first. Where do you start and stop? Where is the finish line? Use the stopwatch in your cell phone to time him. Record the time. In a week or two get him to do it again and see if he improves or declines. Do it every month or so and watch his satisfaction as he improves.

GOING TO BED

One place to get close is when young boys go to bed. When a parent is present to tuck him in it's as if you are on the same team. He has the covers pulled up and feels all tucked in and likely feels safe. It is this moment that sometimes boys will tell you what is on their mind. Things are quiet, no one else is around, they have a sense of safety and all of these things create a safe place for him. He may not say a thing but then again he might. As parents we want to be there at times like this and be ready and open if he is interested in bringing up issues or problems that he is facing that he might usually not talk about. On the other hand just being there with him, and without talking is a real blessing for him. Your presence and attention is part of what he strives for. Be very aware of the possibility that he may bring things up in a very indirect manner. He may not start by talking about himself, he may start by talking about a friend who has problems. Listen closely and ask open-ended questions.

COMING HOME FROM SCHOOL

Another time that is similar and worked great for me when my kids were young is when they come home from school. If you meet them as they come in the door and have a snack ready you are providing a safe place. I have seen this repeatedly. When boys first hit the door as they come home they will tell you everything. But you must be there the moment they come in. Ten minutes later and it won't work. If you catch them in that magical transition between school and home you may hear things that you might not hear otherwise. Most parents don't have that luxury but if you can swing it I think you will find a time where he feels safe and will be more willing to tell you the stories of the day. Another thing to keep in mind is that boys will rarely want to tell the same story twice. If he opens up to dad when he comes home from school he may not want to repeat the same stories again. Dad will likely have to relay the stories directly to mom.

Keep in mind too that if you have to ask questions make them open ended. By that I mean to ask things like "What was the best part of your day today?" or "which of your friends makes you laugh the hardest and how does he do it?" These can't be easily answered with a yes or a no. They require at least a couple of words and that can get things started. Remember, avoid questions about emotions unless you know he is interested in making that a part of the discussion.

Yet another potential safe place for young boys is riding in the car. This one is much more tricky since there are a number of boys who find the car to be less then a safe place. But there are many boys who will tell you many things when just the two of you are riding in the car together. It's a place they may feel safe. Think of your own son and whether this may or may not be the case with him.

These are all starting ideas about where boys might feel safe. As a parent there is no one who knows your boys better than

Getting Close to Boys

you. You know if your son is athletic and if so, take him to the local high school track and as you walk, he can run. He can watch the older boys work out and will likely enjoy his time there. You know if your son is a more logical thinking type, if so, be sure to do puzzles together or separately. Challenge him with some tough ones. You know if your son is a creative type, if so, do creative things together. You can use your knowledge to help you find out where your boys might feel safe and then see if you can find ways to join them shoulder to shoulder in that safety. When we can do that we are succeeding at getting close.

BOYS AND DISCIPLINE

One of the areas I have seen a great deal of struggle between mothers and sons are in the area of discipline. These struggles, if they get out of control can ruin closeness in a microsecond so it is worth talking a little about discipline. Everyone has their own style of discipline so we will stick to general ideas about what might work better for boys given their unique nature.

So how are boys different when it comes to discipline? First lets look at their ways when it comes to rules. In boy's games the conventional wisdom says that boys want three things. They want to know what the rules are, they want to know who is enforcing those rules, and they want to know that the rules will be enforced fairly. If you have ever watched a group of boys playing a team game without referees or adult supervision you have probably witnessed the boys arguing over the rules. This is standard fare. One observer watched hundreds of boys' games and marveled at the amount of time they took in arguing over the rules. They did it regularly and they did it with passion! The observer also noted that they would almost always come to a conclusion and the game would go on. She compared it with girls' games she had watched where arguments were much more likely to end in one or more of the players quitting and going home and the game coming to an end. Not so with the boys. It seems the arguments over the rules are almost as important as the game itself. In fact, the rules are a part of the system of the game and boys are highly interested in making the system of the game fair and functional.

KNOW WHAT THE RULES ARE

How can you make boy's interest in knowing the rules work for you? One strategy I've seen is parents who include boys in the making of rules for the family. Give the boys a voice. You will maintain your parental final say but having them involved in the conversation about rules can have a very positive impact. When your sons feel that they are a part of the process they are much more likely to "buy in." They feel the rules are theirs and this puts a very different spin on the experience, particularly when they have agreed that the rules are fair. The rule making process can be laborious and time consuming just like the boy's arguments during the games but it is important for you to have agreements about what is acceptable and what is not. Things are likely to go better when boys know the rules.

You can also go a step farther and ask the boys what sorts of consequences they think are appropriate for a breakage of the rules. My experience with this is the boys will choose a much harsher consequence and this needs to be tempered, but you be the judge and see how this works out. When boys have helped set the rules and are also involved in the planning of the consequences it will likely make your job as a parent considerably easier.

I have also found that for older boys who have committed a larger offense it is very helpful to ask them to name the

Boys and Discipline

consequence for their misdeed. Ask them what would help them learn to not do that again and see what they come up with. Sometimes they will offer an idea that you may not have thought of and you think will be fitting. Then again, I have seen it also go the other way. Again, as the parent you are where the buck stops.

It can be very tricky to both create the rules and to agree on the consequences. Set them too high and you will have a tough time enforcing them, set them too low and the consequences lose any real power. Take your time with this. It is important. When boys know the rules things will often go smoother.

Now think about an adult refereed game that boys are playing. The boys know the rules. They know that if they pull on a wide receiver's jersey when he is trying to catch the ball they will be called for pass interference. They also know the punishment, or in this case, the penalty. They may argue about whether the call is correct but they will nearly always respect the call and continue playing the game. What does the ref do when there is an infraction? They announce the penalty and mark off the consequences.

We will likely never see the following interchange of a ref and a player: During a football game a referee sees a defensive player commit a pass interference penalty as he pulls on the jersey of the receiver. The ref goes up to the defensive player and says, "Why are you treating #81 like that? Only a low life would pull a play like that. What a jerk you are."

The ref has now made things personal. He is reacting emotionally to the infraction. This is a mistake I have seen from many parents. Taking it very personally. How could he do that to me? Why would he want to hurt me like that? And a hundred other inner thoughts that parents might have to their son's acting out. Can you see how silly the ref would look? Can you see how his effectiveness would be severely compromised? His power is in watching carefully and calling a foul when he sees it and marking off the penalty. Remember, the good ref calls the foul and marks off the penalty. He doesn't make it personal. He doesn't berate the player, he just marks off the yards. As parents it is hard to not take things personally. Nearly impossible. But keeping this idea in mind may help in limiting your own personal reaction and make things about your son and his infraction rather than being about your hurt.

GO WITH POSITIVE REINFORCEMENT WHEN YOU CAN

Remember living in a hierarchy leaves one with a sense of wanting to come out looking good. Boys thrive on looking good and will work to get accolades. Have him work towards goals where he can succeed and get acknowledged for his effort and his success.

I remember when I was little my mother was frustrated with my not taking out the trash. It was my job. I would let it slip now and then. Then one day she started intermittently putting quarters underneath the trashcans that needed emptying. I discovered this and became more interested in my trash responsibility! She had succeeded in finding a way to positively reinforce my chore. It worked, at least for a while. This example is not meant to be taken as a literal suggestion, it is likely outdated in today's world. But it does give us an idea about how to put a positive spin on a chore that might otherwise be dull and uninviting.

Boys and Discipline

Here's an idea. Each week you have a chores lottery. A chore from one of your children is selected and sealed in an envelope. At the end of the week you open the envelope and whichever of your children had that chore, they get the prize. (money, ice cream, whatever.) But here's the catch. They are only eligible for the lottery if they completed the chore that was in the envelope. If they didn't do that chore they get no prize. This is a way to pair positive reinforcement with getting the chores done.

CHALLENGE HIM

One idea if your son is failing to make his bed regularly is to turn it into a competition. Challenge him. Tell him you bet he can't make his bed in 45 seconds. If he balks, make the bet sweeter and tell him if he can do it in 45 seconds he will get some special treat. See what happens. Think of other challenges you might offer. Boys like a challenge and it fits right in with their competitive hierarchical ways. Tell him that if he makes his bed each day at the end of the week he will get some sort of prize. He is more likely to work towards a prize. Make it work for you.

GIVE HIM AS MUCH RESPONSIBILITY AS YOU CAN

The more responsibility you can give him the better. All too often we strip our children of responsibility when they fail in some way. Boys need to be challenged with more and more responsibility. Find ways to make him in charge of this or that. Heck - give him a title of some sort. Parents often say that they

Helping Mothers Be Closer to Their Sons

don't want their sons to fail and so they avoid giving him responsibility. I think the opposite is correct. We want our sons to fail while they are under our watch. It won't be long before he is on his own. Much better to fail now under your loving hands where you can help him see the failure and adjust. Much better to fail now than to fail when he is on his own. Plus if you give him more responsibility he can wear that as a badge of success. Give him chances to win whenever you can.

USE HIS INTEREST IN COMPETITION

You know now that he is likely competitive. Make that work for you. Set up possible competitions that will work in your favor. Here's an example:

You have two sons. Tell them that if they both get all their chores done by Friday that they will get a certain reward. Make it something they both want. What you will likely see, if the reward is something they really want, is they will work together to get things done and will likely be urging each other on.

There's a private boys' school outside of Washington DC, the Mater Dei School, that uses boys' competitive nature to help in both deportment and scholarship. They divided the school into two groups, the Blues and the Whites. When you enroll in that school you are assigned either to the white or the blue team. From that point forward everything you do creates points for or against your team. If you get straight A's, your team benefits, do more community service, your team benefits. If you excel in sports or extra-curricular activities your team gets points. The rivalry is fierce. The boys push each other to get more points and when they have more points they get both special privileges

Boys and Discipline

and bragging rights. Needless to say, the boys do much of the policing and the grades are top notch. Compare this to our default public schools that have removed competition from the curriculum. Schooling has become increasingly buffered from all things competition. The focus is not on who is first, second and third, the focus is on getting along, being nice to each other, and staying quiet. It doesn't take much to notice where the boys are doing better. Give them some competition.

This school also awards a young boy once a week with the school prize for best school citizen. The boys strive to get the award. The older boys also have an award but theirs is monthly and rather than be decided by the teachers and administrators, the older boys vote on a winner among their peers. This school is very wise in giving boys the opportunity to succeed with recognition and also giving the older boys more responsibility for their own behavior and evaluation of their peers. My hat is off to this school.

Good luck with your boys.

ADOLESCENCE

Adolescence brings a real challenge for parents, especially for mothers and sons. Robert Moore, a Jungian Analyst and theorist said once, "The goal of the adolescent is to kill the parent and the goal of the parent is to not retaliate."[35] I have yet to meet a parent who heard this idea and didn't chuckle and shake their head. It speaks a certain truth that is missing in our culture. The adolescent is working hard to individuate and become their own person. Their closeness and allegiance is shifting away from the family and toward their peers. They are working towards being independent that is complicated by their urge to go back to the safety of being a ten year old. This push towards independence and leaving the familiar and safe ties of the family is a very difficult time for both parent and adolescent and there are very few supports for parents in this struggle.

In other cultures there are rituals that bring this very difficult transition to light and into our conscious awareness. Here's an example of a ritual that is used in another culture to help the boys leave the mother when the time is right.

The mother asks the son to go and get her a cup of water from the well. The son obeys her and comes back with the water and throws it into her face. He then walks off to be with the men.[36]

Helping Mothers Be Closer to Their Sons

This is a ritual that marks this transition. I have related this to a number of mothers who understood all too well the sense that their son had thrown water in her face. They surely don't like it but they also know that feeling. This is what it feels like and it hurts, but seeing this as a life transition and not just as a personal insult can help mitigate the hardest edges of this transition.

Another ritual involves the boys and mothers:

The moms and boys were doing their usual things in the village when out of nowhere a group of masked invaders enter their space and select certain boys and carry them away from the village. The mothers give chase screaming at these masked monsters to bring their sons back but the monsters will do no such thing no matter how much the mothers scream. The monsters run off with the boys at full speed. The women give up and head back to the village and relax and talk and laugh. They knew this one was coming and the boys who were of age were carried off to be with only the men. The ladies could relax and have a cup of tea.[37]

Both of these rituals point to a very difficult period for moms when the boys are adolescents. This is when boys really need to be with their fathers and give moms a rest. Sadly the opposite is happening all too often with fathers being removed from the homes in today's world. Do what you can to help your son have time with his father. If it can't be with his father maybe an uncle. If not an uncle, find a male that cares about him and encourage contact.

BOYS AND EMOTIONS —
SOME TIPS

When boys are young, start them off by teaching them the four basic emotions: Sad, mad, glad, and afraid. Nearly all of the many variations of emotions fall under those four basic feelings. They are also easy to memorize since they rhyme. Teach him the basics of each one. What it is like when you are sad, mad, glad or afraid. Try to do this when the environment is calm. Keep in mind that the boy's brain may be handicapping him when it comes to connecting words and emotions. As we have seen, testosterone does seem to be involved in this. It is interesting that there may be evolutionary value in his difficulty with emotions. Men and boys have evolved over the eons with the role of protecting the perimeter and guarding the compound. What does this task require? It requires someone who will pull the trigger if need be no matter what. It could easily be argued that emotions would simply get in the way of this critical action and therefore men and boys have evolved to put making that decision first based on logic and emotions second, or third. So when you are working with boys and their emotions keep that in mind.

Helping Mothers Be Closer to Their Sons

Help him see that whenever he wonders what he might be feeling he can just ask himself is it one of those four, sad, mad, glad, or afraid. It usually will be one of those and he can start to have success in putting his emotions into words at least in his own mind.

The other thing you can do to help is to get him to connect his bodily experience with the emotion. Boys are usually very aware of their bodies and this can be a great way to help them understand their emotions. Show him that when he is angry he will likely hold his breath a bit, will likely clinch his fists and have tension in his upper body and jaw. When he is anxious show him that his breath will be quick and shallow, and he may feel a little shaky and timid. When he is glad show him that everything is pointing up! Literally. Watch football players after a touchdown and you will see that they are pointing up, bouncing up in the air etc. Everything is up, high fives and all. Note also that the opposing team is looking downward, feeling the weight and burden of gravity. When we are sad the pull of gravity is heavy, we don't want to move, and we can feel stuck. By learning the body correlates of emotions, he will be in a much better place to understand his emotions and identify them through his body experience. I have used this in my practice with adolescent males many times. They come in with a great deal of emotion but are having are hard time becoming conscious of what they are feeling. I just ask them what they are feeling in their body and they start explaining in detail. My arms are tight, my jaw is tight, or my upper body is tight. I'm just tight. Then a simple question like, when someone is feeling tight like that, what might they be feeling? Then bingo! Often times the realization is so sudden he will shout, "I'm Pissed", with great satisfaction. He realizes he is angry and starts making connections.

Boys and Emotions

It will be much easier to ask your young son about what he is feeling in his body. Asking about emotions directly will usually end in frustration. He will likely respond positively to the body question but not so positively to the feeling oriented question. Not because he doesn't want to tell you the answer but because he doesn't understand. This is at least in part the case since the emotions are confusing for him and admitting that will drop him in the hierarchy. Talking about his body is a much safer place. Just ask him, "What are you feeling in your body right now?" This is a non-threatening question for boys and may help to get the conversation going. Keep in mind that some boys will have a very easy time in naming and discussing emotions while others will be stumped. Know where your son falls in this area and adjust your interactions based on his strengths.

Another idea that helps with boys is to use a 1-10 scale. You can use it for everything, i.e. "So how was your day at school, give me a one to ten." "How are you feeling about your homework, one to ten?" Tell him one is the worst and ten is the best. He will tell you a number that matches with his day or homework and that is an opening to hear more. "You were an 8 yesterday and a 6 today, what happened to drop you the two points?" The point system is much easier to talk about than feelings. It is also hierarchical which likely plays to his strengths. Be sure to model this behavior and give him a number for how your day went. It can also be fun

Summary and Resources

Boys face multiple factors that are too often overlooked, leaving boys misunderstood.

We began looking at three factors that impact boys psychologically and physically: the testosterone flood, male on male competition and precarious manhood. We described the ways those three influenced boys. The testosterone flood changes his brain to what is called a masculine brain and makes it more likely he will be attracted to women, be more "systems" oriented, be more aggressive, and like "guy" stuff. These changes are variable depending on the amount of testosterone he received in utero, are permanent, and last a lifetime. We then looked at how boys are immersed in male-to-male competition from an early age. Fueled from within by testosterone, they practice this in their play as boys and then manifest the competition as adults. As these two factors push boys from within, precarious manhood pushes boys from the outside. The push is to repeatedly prove he is a man. Boys and men are aware that they are judged continually and strive to put their best foot forward to ensure that others see them as men.

Helping Mothers Be Closer to Their Sons

We then had a look at how boys have been able to adjust to the following three attributes. First we looked at how and why they worked to keep their emotions invisible, and followed that by examining their ways to heal. Finally, we saw how they are very clever in using action and inaction to tell their story and use these experiences to slowly process their emotions.

We turned then to have a look at a number of ways to get close to them including shoulder to shoulder activities, storytelling, and sometimes just "being" with them. Following that we had a quick look at discipline, adolescence and teaching boys about emotions.

We have only touched the tip of the iceberg. I am hoping that you will find this book's contents interesting enough to seek out further knowledge on this fascinating topic. There is a great deal more to learn about boys and how they live their lives. Below is a list of resources that you may find helpful on your quest to learn even more about boys.

At the top of the list would have to be the following:

Male, Female: The Evolution of Human Sex Differences - David Geary

This text was instrumental in helping me gather the information for this book. It is an academic text but is written in such a friendly manner that it is very easy to read and understand. Geary goes into great detail examining the research on the evolution of our sex differences. I highly recommend this book.

The Essential Difference - Simon Baron-Cohen

Another excellent volume that is well written and packed with helpful information. Baron-Cohen's book is very carefully

Summary and Resources

crafted not to offend the politically correct but it still offers great information and insight into our differences. His focus is on empathic versus systems oriented brains.

Brain Gender - Melissa Hines

This one is also worth checking out. Hines's research appears throughout this book. She is a creative and prolific researcher and her book is packed with information on our brain differences.

Other books that you might find helpful include:

Raising Boys - Steve Biddulph

This is an older book but is refreshing in its ability to ignore the politically correct aspect of things. It is more a handbook on tips for raising boys. Biddulph is Australian so there may be some cultural differences but still worth having a look.

Boys Adrift – Len Sax

Sax does a great job of looking at the crisis boys face in today's world. He looks into ADHD medications, boys' education, endocrine disruptors and more.

The Wonder of Boys - Michael Gurian

This is a classic on boys. Originally written in 1996, it is still worth reading. Gurian has written quite a few helpful books on boys.

Real Boys - William Pollack

Another classic filled with good information on the uniqueness of boys.

Helping Mothers Be Closer to Their Sons

The Boy Crisis - Warren Farrell

New as of 2016 and continues in Farrell's tradition of being exceedingly well written and helpful. Farrell has a way of taking a very complex problem and putting it into words that are easy to understand. Looks into the elements of the boy crisis, and how boys are facing difficulties that most of us don't see.

My Grief Journal, for kids

This is an Ipad app put together by John Lemasters specifically for tech savvy grieving children. A perfect match for boys. Free download.

The Way Men Heal - Tom Golden

I couldn't help but mention my own books. This one is not specifically on boys but tells the story of men and boys' healing.

Swallowed by a Snake: The Gift of the Masculine Side of Healing - Tom Golden

Originally written in the 1990's it remains a standard for grieving people to understand the sex differences in the ways we heal and serves as a map for men into the process of healing.

REFERENCES

1. Connellan, Jennifer, Simon Baron-Cohen, Sally Wheelwright, Anna Batki, and Jag Ahluwalia. "Sex Differences in Human Neonatal Social Perception." *Infant Behavior and Development* 23.1 (2000): 113-18. Web.

2. Baron-Cohen, Simon. The Essential Difference: The Truth about the Male and Female Brain. New York: Basic, 2003. Print.

3. Ibid.

4. Hines, Melissa, Michaela Constantinescu, and Debra Spencer. "Early Androgen Exposure and Human Gender Development." *Biology of Sex Differences* 6.1 (2015): n. pag. Web.

5. Eaton, Warren O., and Lesley R. Enns. "Sex Differences in Human Motor Activity Level." *Psychological Bulletin* 100.1 (1986): 19-28. Web.

6. Ibid.

7. Arnold, A. "Organizational and Activational Effects of Sex Steroids on Brain and Behavior: A Reanalysis." *Hormones and Behavior* 19.4 (1985): 469-98. Web.

8. Alexander, Gerianne M. "Postnatal Testosterone Concentrations and Male Social Development." *Frontiers in Endocrinology* 5 (2014): n. pag. Web.

9. Goy, R. "Behavioral Masculinization Is Independent of Genital Masculinization in Prenatally Androgenized Female Rhesus Macaques."*Hormones and Behavior* 22.4 (1988): 552-71. Web.

10. University of Virginia Health System. "Sex Chromosome Genes Influence Aggression And Maternal Behavior, Say Researchers." ScienceDaily. ScienceDaily, 7 March 2006. <www.sciencedaily.com/releases/2006/03/060306214707.htm>.

11. Eisenegger, Christoph, Johannes Haushofer, and Ernst Fehr. "The Role of Testosterone in Social Interaction." Trends in Cognitive Sciences15.6 (2011): 263-71. Web.

12. Tanner, J. M. *Foetus into Man: Physical Growth from Conception to Maturity*. Cambridge, MA: Harvard University Press, 1978. Print.

13. Geary, David C. *Male, Female: The Evolution of Human Sex Differences*. Washington, DC: American Psychological Association, 2010. 59-61. Print.

14. Geary, David C. *Male, Female: The Evolution of Human Sex Differences*. Washington, DC: American Psychological Association, 2010. 219-220. Print.

15. Geary, David C. *Male, Female: The Evolution of Human Sex Differences*. Washington, DC: American Psychological Association, 2010. 78-79. Print.

References

16. National Public Radio. "Testosterone." *This American Life,* n.d. Web. 06 Jan. 2016.

17. Savin-Williams, Ritch C. *Adolescence: An Ethological Perspective.* New York: Springer-Verlag, 1987. Print.

18. Maccoby, Eleanor E., and Carol Nagy Jacklin. "Gender Segregation in Childhood." *Advances in Child Development and Behavior Advances in Child Development and Behavior* 20 (1987): 239-87. Web.

19. Geary, David C. *Male, Female: The Evolution of Human Sex Differences.* Washington, DC: American Psychological Association, 2010. 322. Print.

20. Hassrick, Royal B., Cile M. Bach, and Dorothy Maxwell. *The Sioux: Life and Customs of a Warrior Society.* Norman, OK: University of Oklahoma, 1964. Print.

21. Geary, David C. *Male, Female: The Evolution of Human Sex Differences.* Washington, DC: American Psychological Association, 2010. 414-415. Print.

22. Ibid.

23. Gilmore, David D. *Manhood in the Making: Cultural Concepts of Masculinity.* New Haven, CT: Yale University Press, 1990. Print.

24. Vandello, Joseph A., and Jennifer K. Bosson. "Hard Won and Easily Lost: A Review and Synthesis of Theory and Research on Precarious Manhood." *Psychology of Men & Masculinity* 14.2 (2013): 101-13. Web.

25. Simon, R. W., and A. E. Barrett. "Nonmarital Romantic Relationships and Mental Health in Early Adulthood: Does the Association Differ for Women and Men?" *Journal of Health and Social Behavior* 51.2 (2010): 168-82. Web.

26. Marin, Peter. "Abandoning Men: Jill Gets Welfare–Jack Becomes Homeless." *The Alicia Patterson Foundation*, 15 Apr. 2-11. Web. 07 Jan. 2016.

27. Golden, Thomas R. *Swallowed by a Snake: The Gift of the Masculine Side of Healing*. Gaithersburg, MD: Golden Healing Publishing, 2000. Print.

28. Wager, Tor D., K. Luan Phan, Israel Liberzon, and Stephan F. Taylor. "Valence, Gender, and Lateralization of Functional Brain Anatomy in Emotion: A Meta-analysis of Findings from Neuroimaging." *NeuroImage* 19.3 (2003): 513-31. Web.

29. Van Honk et al. "Testosterone Administration Impairs Cognitive Empathy in Women Depending on Second-to-fourth Digit Ratio." *Proceedings of the National Academy of Sciences* 110.28 (2013): 11660-1661. Web.

30. Eisenegger, Christoph, Michael Naef, Romana Snozzi, Markus Heinrichs, and Ernst Fehr. "Prejudice and Truth about the Effect of Testosterone on Human Bargaining Behaviour."*Nature* 463.7279 (2009): 356-59. Web.

31. Valerio, Max W. *The Testosterone Files: My Hormonal and Social Transformation from Female to Male*. Emeryville, CA: Seal, an Imprint of Avalon Publishing Group, 2006. Print.

32. Panksepp, Jaak, and Lucy Biven. *The Archaeology of Mind: Neuroevolutionary Origins of Human Emotions*. New York: W. W Norton, 2012. Print.

References

33. Taylor, Shelley E. The Tending Instinct: How Nurturing Is Essential for Who We Are and How We Live. New York: Times, 2002. Print.

34. Greene, Bob. *Rebound: The Odyssey of Michael Jordan.* Darby, PA: Diane Publishing Company, 1995. Print.

35. Moore, Robert. A Study in Masculine Psychology, audio tape series, King, Magician Warrior, Lover. C.G.Jung Institute of Chicago, 1989.

36. Eliade, Mircea, and Willard R. Trask. *Rites and Symbols of Initiation: The Mysteries of Birth and Rebirth.* New York: Harper & Row, 1965. Fin Print.

37. Ibid

ABOUT THE AUTHOR

Thomas Golden, LCSW is well known in the field of healing from loss. His first book, Swallowed by a Snake: The Gift of the Masculine Side of Healing has been acclaimed by Elisabeth Kubler-Ross and others. His second book The Way Men Heal has updated the Snake book and added the latest biological differences. Tom enjoys giving workshops in the United States, Canada, Europe, and Australia, having been named the 1999 International Grief Educator by the Australian Centre for Grief Education.

Drawing on thirty years of practical, hands-on clinical experience, Tom brings a gentle sense of humor and a gift for storytelling to both his workshops and his writing. His work and his web site webhealing.com have been featured in the New York Times, the Washington Post, and U.S. News and World Report, as well as on CNN, CBS Evening News, ESPN and the NFL Channel. Tom served as the vice-chair for the Maryland Commission for Men's Health and has also enjoyed helping write a proposal for a White House Council on Boys and Men. whitehouseboysmen.org. He is in private practice in Gaithersburg, MD and also enjoys doing Skype consults. Tom's newest site thewaymenheal.com is a membership site that offers videos on the topic of the way men heal.

Contact

Tom offers workshops on numerous topics including helping mothers be close to sons, the way men heal, consults for hospitals and clinics around the issues of the masculine side of healing and others. He also has consults for individuals online that can be related to the above issues or general coping with life issues. To contact Tom for a consultation or workshop you can use the links below.

WORKSHOPS -- http://webhealing.com/ws.html

CONSULTATIONS-- http://tgolden.com/online-consults

To get a free look at Tom doing videos here's a link: http://tgolden.com/free

If you like the free videos there are plenty more available at the VIDEO ARCHIVE: http://thewaymenheal.com

Email
golden@webhealing.com

Address:
849 Quince Orchard Blvd Ste I
Gaithersburg, MD 20878

Twitter - trgolden

www.ingramcontent.com/pod-product-compliance
Lightning Source LLC
Chambersburg PA
CBHW061450040426
42450CB00007B/1303